D75895
25.⁰⁰

South Africa

South Africa

Photography and text
by Rainer Waterkamp

Paradise at Continent's End

Table of Contents

12 The Land at the Cape of Good Hope

- 14 Landscapes of South Africa
- 16 The "Rainbow Nation"
- 17 The Cradle of Humankind
- 20 *Historical Dates and Pictures*
- 25 The Beginning of "White" History
- 26 Apartheid and Homelands
- 28 *As Diverse as the Land Itself: Cuisine at the Cape*
- 32 Traveling in Another World
- 38 *From Magnificent Blossoms to Desert Vegetation: The Flora of South Africa*

African woman selling her goods in Mtubatuba.

40 Wine Country at the Cape

- 43 A View of Two Oceans
- 45 Peaceful Small Towns in the Wine Country
- 50 *A Diversity of Building Styles: Cape Architecture*
- 52 An Excursion to the "French Corner"
- 52 European Traditions along the "Wine route"
- 54 The Stifling Atmosphere of Apartheid has Vanished
- 58 *Fine Vintages: The Wines of South Africa*

Montagu – a renowned wine-growing region in the Little Karoo.

60 Plantations, Primeval Forests and Fantastic Beaches

- 62 The Garden Route and Little Karoo
- 66 Glittering Landscape – The Lake District
- 70 *A Fashion Outlasting the Centuries: Ostriches – Breeding and Farms*
- 72 Bathing Beaches and Fairytale Forests
- 73 The "Detroit of South Africa"
- 78 *An Expression of Tribal Identity: The Art of the Ndebele*

Wilderness – here there are superb sand beaches.

80 Corridors of Rock and the "Dragon's Ridge"

- 80 Settler's Country – A Little Piece of England in the Land of the Xhosa
- 83 Cliffs and Lonely Bays – The Wild Coast
- 85 Boomtown Durban
- 86 The "Dragon's Ridge" – The Drakensberg
- 90 *The "Switzerland of Africa": The Kingdom of Lesotho*
- 94 Natal Midlands and Valley of 1000 Hills
- 96 Game Reserves and Tourism
- 100 *The Kingdom of Swaziland: Ngawane*

The Drakensberg – a symphony of brilliant colors.

102 Cities, Pasturelands, Waterfalls

- 106 Voortrekker Mentality in the Shade of Jacaranda Blossoms
- 108 Venda – Land of the Rain Queen
- 109 On the Panorama Route
- 112 *From Hunting Preserve to Protected Area: The Kruger National Park*
- 118 Boer Traditions in Managuang
- 122 *A Last Paradise: Endangered Botswana*

Leopards – a member of the Big Five that is seldom seen

124 Sandstone Arches and Wild Flowers

- 126 Wild Flowers in Namaqualand
- 129 Tea, Sheep and Rock Drawings
- 134 *The "Big Five": Rulers of the Animal World*
- 136 The Place of Great Noise – Augrabies Falls
- 136 Sultanas, Port and Sherry
- 138 The Land of Red Dunes – The Kalahari
- 142 *German Footprints in the Sand – A Detour to Namibia*

*Augrabies Falls –
here the Oranje River drops into a deep gorge.*

144 Planning your Journey

- 147 *Metropolis at Table Mountain: The Best Walking Tour of Cape Town*
- 148 *A Wildlife Paradise for Tourists: The Most Beautiful National Parks at a Glance*
- 152 *Discovering the Land at the Cape: The Five Most Scenic Routes*

Unforgettable – the dune landscape of the Kalahari.

156 People, Places, Topics

The meat of the male waterbuck tastes so unpleasant that other predators do not touch it (above). – African elephants are larger than their Asian counterparts, and their ears are also larger. The herds consist of 10 to 20 animals but may comprise up to 50 elephants and are constantly on the move, seeking forage; they require 250 kg of food per day, in addition to minerals and a supply of water. Furthermore, they love to bathe in mud pools; a herd in Addo Elephant National Park (right).

Magnificent beaches fringe the coast road east of Cape Town.

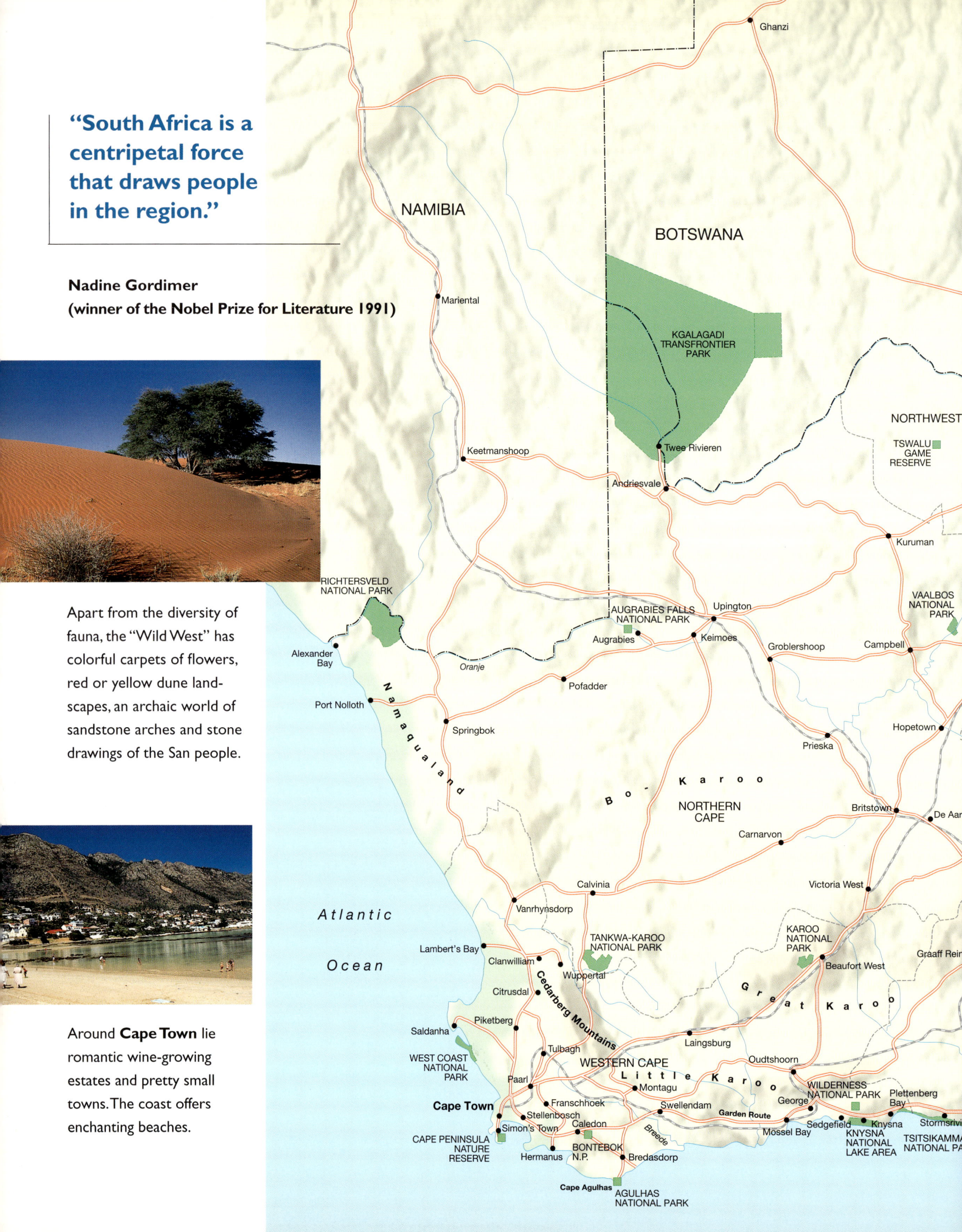

> "South Africa is a centripetal force that draws people in the region."

Nadine Gordimer
(winner of the Nobel Prize for Literature 1991)

Apart from the diversity of fauna, the "Wild West" has colorful carpets of flowers, red or yellow dune landscapes, an archaic world of sandstone arches and stone drawings of the San people.

Around **Cape Town** lie romantic wine-growing estates and pretty small towns. The coast offers enchanting beaches.

Endless wheat fields, interspersed with old towns, characterize the **Boer Country**. The Blyde River Canyon with its waterfalls and the sparsely populated land of the Rain Queen could not be more picturesque. The fertile plateau and the Kruger National Park are only a few of the highlights of this region.

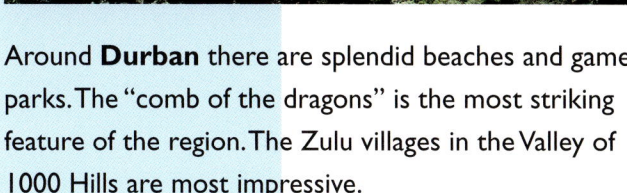

Around **Durban** there are splendid beaches and game parks. The "comb of the dragons" is the most striking feature of the region. The Zulu villages in the Valley of 1000 Hills are most impressive.

The Land at the Cape of Good Hope

Increasing settlement, the growing rural exodus and the penetration of Western civilization have destroyed much of the older cultural heritage, but in particular the artistically-minded Ndebele (above) and the war-like Zulu (right) have largely maintained their cultural identity. – The Epupa Falls in Namibia (right-hand page) here represent a grandiose natural world that is under threat from civilization.

Breathtaking landscapes and a diversity of peoples; pulsating cities and idyllic settlements; vast farms with lush, waving fields of corn and wheat, tall sugar cane plantations and green vineyards; National Parks with exemplary nature and animal conservation policies – South Africa is a destination that offers travelers not only variety but also a relaxing vacation, interesting experiences and luxury-standard comfort. The country can be easily explored, for although it lies in the Third World, it has all the amenities of civilization and an excellent infrastructure, making travel a pleasant undertaking. A large number of first-class hotels and restaurants attract guests as do the renowned galleries, theaters and museums in the modern cities. Charming Dutch Cape villas and colonial architecture are a source of admiration, and so are the shining skyscrapers and comfortable lodges. The dream of evenings by the campfire can be experienced as easily as romantic sunsets or the endless expanse of the savannas. South Africa is a paradise for lovers of nature and sports, for hobby and professional photographers, and for those fascinated by foreign cultures. Sun-worshippers, fans of sporting activities and gourmets enjoying festive menus in cozy farmhouses will all find exactly what they are seeking.

Cocooned in the comfort and safety of a lodge, nature in Africa seems remarkably innocuous. To the eyes of visitors weary of civilization, it appears larger than life, as on a wide cinema screen. Only when you are not permitted to move around the grounds of the lodge without an armed guard as escort do you have the first inkling that the wilderness in this country can still be dangerous.

Landscapes of South Africa

The national flower of South Africa is the king protea or sugarbush (right-hand page). The blossom of the jacaranda trees envelops the capital city, Pretoria, in a mauve-colored sea of blooms (right). – In Kirstenbosch National Botanical Gardens in Cape Town, one can admire many of the numerous flowers and plants of the country (large photo).

"A whole world in one country," as promised by the slogan of the South African tourist office, is a fitting description of the multi-faceted appearance of the country. Over millions of years it has been uniquely shaped by nature, as if it was indeed creating a microcosm of all its aspects. South Africa has some of the oldest geological formations in the world. Since the early Paleozoic period more than 560 to 230 million years ago it has been part of a continental land mass, the heart of the former Gondwanaland. When that broke apart and South America became separated from Africa about 130 million years ago, lava flows streamed across the country and the subcontinent formed an enormous

Olive Schreiner – an Artist against War

The little town of Cradock between Graaf Reinet and Mountain Zebra National Park was the home of the artist Olive Emilie Schreiner, who was born on March 24, 1855 as the daughter of a German missionary in Witteberge (in present-day Lesotho). In 1870, she moved to the area near Cradock, where she worked as a governess for a Boer family. In 1881, she went to live in England. There she published her feminist novella, "Story of an African Farm" in 1883 under the pseudonym Ralph Iron. In 1894, she married a farmer, Samuel Cronwright. During the Boer War she was banished to an internment camp by Cecil Rhodes (1853–1902) because she had criticized the British war strategies in her book "Trooper Peter Halket of Mashonaland," published in 1897, and in "An English South African Woman's View of the Situation" (1899). She wrote of the "stupid and arrogant racial policies and the white occupation and rule by force." She died in Wynberg/Cape Town on December 10, 1920. The Olive Schreiner House in Cradock is now a museum and open to visitors.

bowl. The high rim was forced back into the interior to the line that today marks the Great Escarpment, leaving only a narrow coastal strip. The results of this tectonic action can be seen on all sides: magnificent coastlines with steep cliffs, endless sandy beaches, lagoons, grassy plains, dunes, deserts and stony semi-deserts, bizarre rock formations, deep gorges, mountain ranges with waterfalls and subtropical regions, as well as rainforests with valuable and rare trees all make up the "whole world in one country." Gentle, undulating plateaus cover the Central Highlands, the highveld that is interrupted in some places only by table mountains or rounded hilly ranges. In the central interior there are bucolic cultivated and pasture landscapes, with isolated farmsteads and endless fields of corn, wheat and sunflowers. And Zululand, largely covered with fields of sugarcane, stretches south from Swaziland to the steep wall of the Drakensberg mountain range.

From the Central Highlands in the north to Botswana, the bushveld drops gradually down to the barren Kalahari, and in the east it falls more abruptly like a steep step to the lowveld and the

Kruger National Park, a region where malaria is prevalent. We should not forget, either, the semidesert expanses of the Great Karoo and the Richtersveld on the west coast, as well as the dry region of Namaqualand that once a year is transformed into a magical colorful carpet of flowers, and which gradually gives way to the Namib Desert with its crimson-red sand dunes.

The "Rainbow Nation"

If South Africa's landscapes are characterized by diversity, its population is no less so. The former Anglican Archbishop Desmond Tutu (born 1931) once called the 42.8 million people of this country the "rainbow people of God." He commented at the time, "that we are now free, all of us, black and white together, we, the rainbow people of God." The population is 77 percent of original African descent, ten percent white, nine percent mixed race of black and white parents, and three percent Asian. But the much propagated "melting pot of the nations" is still only a dream. In this part of the world as elsewhere, the peoples and cultures still live side by side rather than being fully integrated. The ethnic variety of the nation is doubtless one of South Africa's tourist attractions, as it represents an interesting mosaic of peoples and traditions. But even the correct designation of the inhabitants poses certain problems, characterized as it frequently is by negative terms of prejudice dating from the colonial period. The designation "Negro" is of course no longer acceptable, but the common term "black" is really only the translation of a French expression. African, the word normally preferred in Africa, is unsuitable for South Africa, as the white Boers used the term "Afrikaner" to mean anyone except the black inhabitants. The word "colored" is also incorrect in South Africa as here this means those of mixed race – Indians, Chinese and other "non-blacks" (coloreds). The term "kaffir", still frequently used for black inhabitants, has a negative touch, of course, but it continues to exist in names like "kaffir buffalo." Even the word "native" should be replaced by the better word "inhabitant" because of the denigrating use of this term during the colonial period; however, this also removes the ethnic distinction. Even the names for the black peoples of South Africa are not uniform and are affected by prejudice. The small, yellow-skinned people are called "San" after their language, which contains many click consonants. This is a more neutral term than the degrading "Bushmen," as the white settlers called them. However, San is a designation of foreign origin, so that recently the name for Bushmen has taken on a new value – all the more so since, following political self-determination, the San frequently actually call themselves bushmen.

When Europeans arrived on the coast of South Africa, they met cattle herders who were called Khoikhoi, after their language, but who were given the name Hottentots by the whites because when they greeted them their gesticulations were accom-

Hotagterklip (left-hand page) is a small village at Cape Agulhas, where fishermen go about their trade (bottom). – From the rocks at the estuary of the Storms River there are magnificent views of the turbulent ocean (large photo).

panied by words that sounded like "hautito." Although the word "khoi" actually means "outcast" or "barbarian", the term is still used generally today instead of Hottentots.

Finally, in all the languages of the large Bantu language group, Bantu actually means simply "the people." But this term has acquired a negative connotation through apartheid, because there were Bantu homelands. Therefore it is only acceptable today as a name for the language. The terms "black" and "white" are indeed more neutral and widely used.

The Cradle of Humankind

Scientists believe that the cradle of mankind lies in Africa. Discoveries of fossilized bones in caves in places such as Taung, Sterkfontein and Makapan prove that early forms of humans known as hominids (Australopithecus = southern primate) existed in Africa between two and three million years ago. In a limestone quarry in Taung near Kimberley, a small skull was found in 1924. The assertion by Professor Raymond Dart of the University of Witwatersrand that this was the skull of a child of a previously unknown type of hominid was initially ignored by the scientific world. The child from Taung was a young Australopithecus africanus.

The Sterkfontein Caves near Johannesburg, 12 kilometers (8 miles) southwest of Krugersdorp on the grounds of the farms Kromdraai and Swartkrans, were discovered in 1896 by an Italian, Guigimo Martinaglia, who was prospecting for gold. They are one of the most significant prehistoric archeological sites in the world. The excavations led by the paleontologist Robert Broom (1866–1951) from the Transvaal Museum and his pupil, John Robinson, led to the discovery of 70 remains of early hominids in Sterkfontein between 1947 and 1949. The skull of an adult Australopithecus africanus discovered in 1947 was affectionately named Mrs. Ples because of its original designation Plesi anthropus transvaalensis. Further investigations, however, proved that it was a male. This skull and part of the hip bones prove that hominids had developed in southern Africa three million years ago, and that they walked upright. In the late 1960s, anthropologists discovered bones

See page 22

The Golden Gate Highlands National Park.

Historical Dates and Pictures

*1 Picture of Cape Town from the year 1683, thirty years after the founding of the colony. –
2 Photograph of Cecil Rhodes, who lived from 1853 to 1902. –
3 Historical picture of the mission church at Groenenkloof. –
4 Xhosa Chief Magomo.
5 Xhosa Chief Sandile.
6 Willem Frederik de Klerk proclaimed the abolition of apartheid in 1990 and opened the way for democracy and Nelson Mandela (7), with whom he shared the Nobel Peace Prize.*

1488: Bartholomeu Dias is the first European to sail around the southern tip of the Cape Peninsula.
1497: Vasco da Gama lands in St. Helena Bay near the Cape.
1510: The Portuguese explorer Francisco d'Almeida, Viceroy of India, disembarks in the bay at Table Mountain to take fresh water on board.
1647: The "Nieuw Haarlem" is stranded near the Cape and 60 people wait for one year at Table Bay to be rescued.
1653–1654: The first Asians are deported to Cape Town. More slaves are brought from West Africa, Java and Madagascar.
1658: First conflicts between white settlers and the Khoikhoi people.
1688: Huguenots arrive at the Cape and found the settlements Franschhoek, Drakenstein (Paarl) and Stellenbosch.

1779: The Trek Boers come into conflict in the east with the Nguni, a Xhosa people, who have settled there. This leads to the so-called Kaffir Wars that last almost 100 years. The wars involve heavy losses and culminate in the conquest of the Xhosa.
1795: The British send a squadron to Cape Town to secure the colony for themselves.
1815: The Congress of Vienna confirms Great Britain's rights to its overseas colony. The Cape lands thus become the first official colony of the British Empire.
1825: English becomes the official language and, from 1827, also the judicial language.
1833: The British abolish slavery in the Cape Colony. Many Boers leave the country and migrate northeastwards.
1852: Transvaal becomes an independent Boer republic. In 1854 the Orange Free State is also granted independence.
1857: Founding of the South African Republic, consisting of Transvaal and the Orange Free State. The region around Lydenburg becomes the independent Lydenburg Republic.
1867: Diamond deposits are discovered at Kimberley, whereupon Great Britain annexes the area which is also claimed by the Orange Free State.
1880–1881: First Boer War between the British and the Boers.
1893: Mahatma Gandhi arrives in Natal and organizes the resistance of Indian immigrants against discriminatory laws.
1899–1902: During the Second Boer War Great Britain annexes the Transvaal and the Orange Free State.

1910: The Union of South Africa is founded.
1931: The Union of South Africa becomes a dominion of the British Commonwealth of Nations.
1948: The National Party wins the elections and subsequently commences the policy of discrimination known as apartheid.
1960: After bloody conflicts in Sharpeville, a national state of emergency is declared. The African National Congress (ANC), founded by the blacks in 1912, is banned.
1961: In a referendum, South Africans vote to leave the Commonwealth. South Africa adopts the name Republic of South Africa.
1962: Nelson Mandela is sentenced to death, later commuted to life imprisonment.
1976: Demonstration by more than 15,000 students in Soweto. The "student uprising of Soweto" goes down in history.
1977: The United Nations (UN) implements a weapons embargo against South Africa.
1986: A national state of emergency is declared. First talks between the government and Mandela.
1989: Frederik de Klerk proclaims the end of apartheid. He repeals the ban on the ANC and other parties. On February 11, Nelson Mandela is released from prison. The state of emergency is lifted and the ANC renounces its armed struggle.
1991: Apartheid is abolished. South Africa prepares for its first general and free elections.
1993: Mandela and de Klerk are awarded the Nobel Peace Prize for their efforts in establishing a democratic South Africa. The assembly of the United Nations votes to lift economic sanctions against South Africa.
1994: South Africa cedes Walvis Bay to Namibia. The ANC wins the first elections in South Africa. Mandela becomes president.
1996: The new constitution is ratified.
1998: Beginning of the hearings of the Truth and Reconciliation Commission.
1999: Nelson Mandela does not stand in the second general election, and Thabo Mvuyelwa Mbeki becomes his successor.
2004: In the third election the ANC and Thabo Mvuyelwa Mbeki are confirmed in power.
2006: The enforced expropriation of about 350 farms is planned within the context of the land reform. By the year 2015, it is intended that approximately 30 percent of South African farmland should pass to black ownership. There are repeated violent, frequently fatal, assaults on white farmers.
2010: South Africa to host the Soccer World Cup.

of modern man, Homo sapiens, who lived around 80,000 years ago in the Klasies River Mouth Caves on the south coast between Cape Town and Port Elizabeth. Early in 1994, two approximately 100,000-year-old fragments of an upper jawbone were discovered in the same caves. These are the oldest known evidence of Homo sapiens who may have migrated from Africa across the whole world. Further traces discovered in Fish Hoek and in the Echo Caves region are aged between 75,000 and 50,000 years. They include bones, tools and rock paintings that are estimated to date from up to 28,000 years BC. Presumably these originated from the San, who along with the Khoikhoi are the oldest known inhabitants of the southern African continent.

In the year 1966, the archaeological site Thulamela (Place of Birth) was opened in the Kruger National Park. It had been discovered by a team led by Maryna Steyn, Coen Nienaber and Marius Loots. The site had been established between 1250 and

The First Explorers and Conquerors

In 1486 Bartholomeu Dias was commissioned by the King of Portugal to find the southern tip of Africa, which he named Cabo Tormentoso (Cape of Storms) because of his bad experiences there. King João II altered the name to Cabo da Bõa Esperança (Cape of Good Hope). In November 1497, Vasco da Gama also sailed around the Cape. Antonio de Saldanha is recorded as the first Portuguese actually to set foot on the Cape in 1503. He is said to have been followed by Francisco d'Almeida in 1510. In 1580, the British buccaneer, Francis Drake, rounded the Cape on his voyage around the globe and described it as the "least dangerous place of our entire circumnavigation."

In 1647, the "Nieuw Haarlem," a Dutch trade ship, sank in Table Bay on its homeward voyage from India. The surviving passengers kept themselves alive by growing vegetables, fishing and bartering for cattle with the native people. The report of one of the survivors of the shipwreck, Leendert Janszen, met with so much interest that the Dutch East India Company decided, as a consequence, to set up a permanent supply station at the Cape.

1 Disembarkation of Jan van Riebeeck in Table Bay of Cape Town in the year 1652. – 2 Adderley Street in Cape Town (postcard). – 3 One hundred years of Johannesburg. – 4 Picture of the Boer Trek. – 5 Depiction (1895) of the construction of the stretch of railroad from Johannesburg to Durban.

1650 by people from the language group of the Shona. A citadel that has been reconstructed from piles of stones is thought to be the oldest structure ever to have been built in South Africa. Other discoveries included jewelry, agricultural tools and porcelain from the Chinese Ming Dynasty. Another find was the skull of a female member of the royal household during the 16th century and the burial place of a possible ruler of Thulamela.

The oldest finds of the predecessors of the people in Transvaal are on a par with the fossils discovered in other African countries, such as Tanzania and Kenya. Skulls found in the Upper Pleistocene layers indicate very early settlement, including the

Behind the ocean promenade of Camps Bay in Cape Town, the mountains known as the "Twelve Apostles" form a scenic backdrop (large photo). – In Stellenbosch there are splendid examples of Cape Dutch architecture (left-hand page, bottom); these include St. Mary's Church (below). – In Cape Town there are numerous statues of historic personalities, for example near City Hall (left).

Paleolithic find at Florisbad near Bloemfontein and the Mesolithic Man of Boskop (Transvaal). They support the thesis that Africa is one of the cradles of humankind – indeed, possibly the principal one.

The Beginning of "White" History

The history of white people in South Africa began when the Portuguese navigator Bartholomeu Dias (ca. 1450–1500) sailed around of the Cape of Good Hope. The Dutch explorer Jan van Riebeeck subsequently founded a supply station for trade ships there in 1652. The indigenous inhabitants were forced to retreat, and in their place slaves from other Dutch colonies were brought into the country. By 1795, more than 20,000 slaves were living in the Cape area. Increasing numbers of Dutch settlers, French Huguenots and Germans arrived, many abandoning crop-growing to become cattle breeders. A new type of farmer grew up, the Trek Boers. They moved into the interior beyond the Drakensberg mountain range, where they encountered the warlike Xhosa and Zulu. Bloody struggles ensued in the Kaffir Wars from 1779 onwards. There was also increasing tension between the authorities at the Cape and the self-confident Trek Boers, who staged an uprising in 1795 in Graaf Reinet and Swellendam before declaring a free republic. In 1814 Holland ceded the Cape to England, causing the Boers to move inland, and in 1838 they killed an estimated 3,000 Zulus at Blood River before founding the Boer Natalia Republic. The might of the great Zulu kingdom created by Shaka

had been destroyed. By 1842, British troops had occupied the harbor at Durban and annexed the hinterland as a crown colony. Shortly afterwards, invading British troops brought the entire territory between the Oranje and Vaal rivers under their control. The independence of the Boers in the areas north of the Vaal was recognized in 1852 and in the areas south of the river in 1854. The two Boer republics, Orange Free State and Transvaal, became sovereign states. However, the situation became more and more critical and in the end led to the Boer War (1899–1902). This had a major influence on the political thinking of white South Africans. For the first time, people died in concentration camps run by the British. In 1910, the Union of South Africa was founded, and in 1931 the Statute of Westminster finally ended British influence.

Apartheid and Homelands

The "Natives Land Act" passed in 1913 designated approximately seven percent of the total area of the country as territories for the black people. These lands formed the heart of the homelands that were enlarged through the "Bantu Land Trust Act" in 1936 to cover 13 percent of the country. The idea of apartheid in a state with many different ethnic groups was not totally illogical. Beginning with Transkei, which was awarded independence in October 1976, ten homelands were intended to become independent states; the many different black peoples were to administer themselves. But the idea had several flaws. For one, the majority of the black people were assigned to numerous widely-scattered areas, while 80 percent of the territory was reserved for whites. For another, economic conditions were miserable in these tracts of land that were long distances apart. In many territories along the east coast (such as KwaZulu, where the Zulus lived, or the Transkei and Ciskei, which were intended for the Xhosa), conditions were at best suited to agriculture, or they degenerated into regions of bitter poverty. The South African government therefore had to pump ever-larger sums of money into these areas, and that frequently landed in the pockets of corrupt government officials and sly profiteers. Furthermore, the industries of "white" South Africa attracted more and more black workers

The huts in the Zulu villages have a dome-shaped roof (above). – Some representatives of the "Rainbow Nation": Himba woman (top), Xhosa woman, married Zulu women and Basotho woman (right-hand page from top left to bottom right).

See page 30

As Diverse as the Land Itself

Cuisine at the Cape

1 The menus of South African restaurants include many dishes with game and tasty seafood, as here in Sandton/Johannesburg.
2 White River is located in a large fruit and vegetable-producing region, as can be seen from the wide variety on offer at the market stalls.
3 An incredible variety of spices can be found at the Indian market in Durban.
4 There is variety, too, on the buffet table on the Phinda Reservation.
5 Zulus offer their guests fresh fruit.

The nation's enormous cultural and ethnic variety is mirrored in the richly varied cuisine of South Africa. Among the most popular local dishes are *braaivleis*, fresh meat grilled on an open fire; *bobotie* (spiced minced lamb); *biltong* (dried beef, Springbok loin, ostrich meat or fish) that is often eaten as a snack between meals; and *boerewors*, a larded peasant sausage made of pork and beef spiced with coriander. *Smoorsnoek* is the name given to steamed fish with onion and potatoes. *Bredie* is a hearty stew of meat and vegetables, flavored with the blossoms of waterblommetjies, which are plants similar to waterlilies. The deep-fried sweet braided dough (*vetkoek*) originated in Holland.
Sosaties are also popular – pieces of mutton, often prepared in a curry marinade and grilled on a skewer. A *leg of Karoo lamb*, roasted slowly in the oven, is seldom served without English *mint sauce*. Usually it is accompanied by sweet potatoes and *butternut* squash, a kind of pumpkin, flavored with cinnamon. Ostrich meat is becoming ever more popular: it tastes good, is lean and delicate and has a low cholesterol content. You will find seafood on virtually every menu in South Africa – for example, smoked or grilled *snoek*, a kind of barracuda, and *klingklip*, which is popular for its firm flesh

and savory taste. *Perlemoen* is the name of a large mussel that actually tastes like veal. Lobster-like crayfish and, of course, oysters are also available. Don't' miss the deep-fried squid *(calamari)*, served with tartare sauce.

Coffee is often served with *koeksisters*, a braided pastry with syrup. The native rooibos tea is made from the twigs of the red bush plant. It has a taste somewhere between black and herbal tea.

Cuisine at the Cape is also influenced by the gastronomic culture of Malaysia, with plenty of curry, chili peppers, cinnamon, cloves and nutmeg. *Samoosas*, spicy pastry triangles filled with curry are especially popular.

The black African style of nutrition is very healthy. Traditionally, plenty of vegetables and fruit are eaten, in addition to dried pulses and grains. A kind of porridge made with boiled maize *(putu)* is also very widespread. Sweet potatoes and pumpkins figure largely in the cuisine of the black population, as do wild spinach and wild melons.

As far as animal products go, milk and poultry are consumed, but beef and goat meat are eaten less frequently. For something adventurous and very nutritious, you can try *masjona* (mopane worms) *tshu-ku* (fried termites) or *xi fu nu nu* (toasted larvae of the scarab beetle).

Water and buttermilk are frequently drunk instead of coffee and tea – and plenty of beer *(maheu)* brewed from millet. Because of its viscosity and unusually sour flavor this is, however, an acquired taste. In the shebeen, the traditional kitchen-bar, Zulu beer *(maheu)* is served.

The local beer has an excellent flavor. White South Africans like long drinks such as brandy and Coke. One local liqueur, *amarula*, is made from the yellow, plum-sized fruits of the marula tree. *Van der hum* is a very sweet, gold-colored liqueur made from mandarin oranges. Local coffee is roasted differently from European coffee and is mixed with chicory.

into the country. There were violent confrontations, resulting in the army being called in, declarations of a state of emergency, arrests and censorship. Gradually it became clear to the government authorities in Pretoria that the idea of the homelands was a mistake. The conflict was exacerbated by racial discrimination, which met with increasing criticism and lack of understanding in the world at large and from Liberal whites within the country. The discrimination of people on the basis of differing skin color was a denial of human rights. Not only were sexual relationships between people of different races forbidden (Immorality Act of 1927); in 1949 a law was passed forbidding marriage between whites and people of other races (Prohibition of Mixed Marriages Act). Other laws decreed that certain professional activities were the sole domain of the whites (Job Reservation). In addition, numerous laws were passed regulating even minor issues of everyday life. These included entrances to buildings, public transport, toilets, accommodation, beaches, events and park benches that were reserved exclusively for whites ("for whites only"). The political conflict culminated in a demonstration against racial passport laws in March 1960, in which 67 people were shot dead by the police. The organizations of the blacks were forbidden and driven underground. In 1963, the police arrested various prominent members of the ANC, including their leader Nelson Mandela (born 1918), who was condemned to lifelong imprisonment. In the year 1976, there were riots in Soweto, the black ghetto of Johannesburg, after the government had resolved to introduce Afrikaans as the educational language in schools. Frederick Willem de Klerk (born 1936) won the 1989 election with promises of reform. In 1990 he announced in Parliament the abolition of apartheid. Nelson Mandela was released after 27 years in prison

Buffalo herd in the Hluhluwe/Umfolozi Game Reserve (large photo) – seabirds at the coast (below, left), hippopotamus with its offspring (left). "Barking" zebras (below).

and cautious discussions began between the ANC and the government. In March 1992, the whites voted by an overwhelming majority to negotiate with the blacks, and, as a consequence, ultimately to relinquish their exclusive power. In May 1992, the "Convention for a Democratic South Africa" was passed by which the homelands Ciskei, Transkei, Bophuthatswana and Venda were reintegrated into South Africa. With the first free general elections the way was opened for peaceful coexistence. On December 10, 1996, in Sharpeville, south of Johannesburg, Mandela placed his signature on the new constitution of South Africa.

The future of South Africa is still uncertain, for the charismatic leader Nelson Mandela, who embodied the new identity of South Africa, has now withdrawn from political life. Fifteen years after the transfer of power, the black population is demanding of the government that they finally fulfill their expectations for a significantly higher standard of living. The most important condition for a flourishing economy remains political stability. But there is still a great contrast between rich and poor corresponding almost identically to white and black. The birth rate among blacks is rising rapidly, and so is unemployment; crime is on the increase. The

Basotho horseman in Lesotho (right). Example of soil erosion (below). – The Blyde River forces its way through the Drakensberg range (bottom). The Epupa Falls in the north of Namibia are a dramatic natural spectacle (large photo).

poverty of the majority of the population may be typical for the Third World, but in South Africa it is confronted with European prosperity, making the discrepancy all the more noticeable.

Traveling in Another World

Anyone who travels in South Africa will experience the African continent with its wild animals at first hand, and yet the visitor from Europe will still be confronted with a feeling of unreality. It is as if everything was just an adventure story on a television or movie screen. The feeling of traveling "in another world" is one that is often experienced in this country. The times in which primitive man had to roll a rock in front of the entrance to his cave in order to be safe from night-time intruders may be long past, but the fear

of wild animals at night-time is still prevalent. The darkness of the African night rouses primeval fears, in spite of all the comforts of civilization that may surround the traveler. For it is still Africa, wild and dangerous Africa. The lion, lying in the grass and seemingly indifferent to the confusion of voices from a whole column of cars laden with tourists taking photographs, is really only waiting for the chance to kill. The hyena that is ducking into a pond is just waiting for the brief moment of inattention on the part of a grazing gazelle; and the powerful bull elephant emerging from the herd which includes young animals with its trunk raised in the air is making an unmistakably threatening gesture. The safari adventure is like a stage play, and yet the fascination of nature is inescapable. African nights can be particularly eerie. Noises from outside the thin walls of a lodge suggest dangers, for example when the roar of the lion sounds through the stillness of the night, or a hyena knocks over the trash can at the edge of the camp. The monotonous humming of insects is interrupted by the cries of the baboons and the hoarse bark of the zebras. During such nights, in the middle of the wilderness, visitors gain an impression of the magnificent but cruel play of nature. The memories that one takes home from a visit to South Africa, a land full of hope after having found its path to prosperity and happiness, are as varied as the land and its people. There are encounters with wild animals and strange peoples; and memories of dangers overcome. And there are memories of dangerous districts in large cities, of the terrible hardship of some people, of the overwhelmingly beautiful, but also merciless nature. In spite of all the social, economic and political problems that characterize South Africa, it is still well worth discovering this land.

The Cape Dutch church of the Rhenish Mission in Stellenbosch has a thatched roof and two neo-classical gables, as well as a double bell tower beside the entrance (below)

Set in the hilly terrain of the Little Karoo are many winegrowing estates, for example, at Montagu (above) and Rhebokskloof, which was named for the antelope (rhebok) that once was indigenous here (right).

Dune landscape in the Kgalagadi Transfrontier Park.

From Magnificent Blossoms to Desert Vegetation

The Flora of South Africa

The protea is the national flower of South Africa. In the region around Cape Town the largest variety of proteas in the world can be found (2). Their blossoms can range from brilliant red to pale green; there are many different forms, for example, "bearded" or "pincushion" (1 and 5) and suikerbos (sugar bush) (3), the most popular variety of protea. – The blue drip disa orchid, which is not found anywhere else in the world, blooms in springtime. Aloe trees (4) grow in the Blyde River region as well as in the former Transkei.

On account of its wide range of climatic regions, South Africa also has a wide variety of vegetation. Savanna (*bushveld*): Savanna vegetation is found in the north along the eastern plateau. This area has a large savanna region, covered with grass and dotted with umbrella thorn acacia and fever tree acacias. The swamp acacia with its yellow-green trunk is particularly striking. The Europeans, who believed that it was a source of malaria, gave it the name "fever acacia." In fact, there is an indisputable link, because the trees, which may reach heights of 25 meters (82 feet), often grow in mosquito-infested swamps. At the edge of the Karoo and the Kalahari, as well as in the bushveld in the west, you will find thorn savanna (dornveld) with predominantly camel thorn acacia and camphor bushes. In the Northern Province/North Transvaal, the vegetation mainly consists of baobab trees, monkey bread trees and candelabra euphorbia. In the south, along the coast of the Indian Ocean, tree euphorbia and elephant bush trees are dominant features.

Grasslands (grassveld): Towards the south-west the savanna gradually gives way to shrub and grass steppe. Grassland or veld is found on the highveld plateau in the eastern interior. Here, trees are found only in gorges and along the rivers.

Karoo vegetation: The bush and grass steppes merge towards the west into the so-called Karoo vegetation, which is also known as dry savanna or semi-desert. The Nama Karoo includes the Karoo region of the Northern Cape Province and extends across the Oranje River to Namibia. The semi-desert vegetation (Karoo) covers almost the entire western interior.

Desert (Succulent Karoo): Genuine desert vegetation with sparse bunch grass, quiver trees or tree aloe and low bushes, such as halfsmenboom succulents ("half-person tree"), is found only along a strip running parallel to the Atlantic coastline and in the north on the border with Namibia. Bushlike succulents and cacti grow primarily in the dry north and in the Northwest Cape Province. The ephemeral carpets of flowers in Namaqualand are among the main natural attractions of South Africa.

Fynbos (Cape Flora): Fynbos vegetation grows in particular in the

the undergrowth of these giants is the cycad, which is said not to have changed since the Jurassic period (150 to 200 million years ago). Palm trees thrive along the subtropical coast of Natal and the Wild Coast. In the swamp areas there are mangrove swamps.

The *botanical world* of South Africa has 22,000 different varieties, of which many are native plants and have been placed under conservation orders. The national flower of South Africa is the protea, which grows in the mountainous areas along with a multitude of lilies and heathers. In addition there are 20 varieties of orchid. Strelitzias and gladioli are both native to South Africa. Daisies form the largest group of wild flowers, comprising more than 2,000 varieties. They can be found in the mountains and along the coast in many bright colors, but they are at their most magnificent in Namaqualand and the Karoo region.

region around the Cape. It consists of more than 8,000 species of plants and survives both hot summers and cold winters equally well. Fynbos consists of three main types of plant – sedge, protea and heather – as well as smaller groups such as pulses or tubers.

Forest vegetation: Evergreen forests with subtropical and tropical characteristics extend along the south coast and on the eastern slopes of the Drakensberg mountains. It is believed that until three million years ago there was a milder climate at the Cape and that subtropical forests existed there. These have survived along the mountains of the Garden Route (Knysna Forest and Tsitsikamma National Park) as well as in KwaZulu-Natal. The mountains here have a completely different flora, including such unusual trees as *yellowwoods* and *stinkwoods*, from which most Dutch Cape style furniture is produced. Hidden in

Wine Country at the Cape

Cape Town and the Cape Region

The Jewish synagogue with Table Mountain in the background (top). – In Company's Garden (right-hand page and above) the first white settlers cultivated fruit and vegetables.

Cape Town is said to be one of the most beautiful cities in the world. Few people will contradict this. The city experiences picture-book weather around 300 days each year, the typical "champagne weather" when the air seems to prickle on the skin. Leendert Janzsen spent a year here in 1647 with the crew of the stranded ship, the "Nieuw Haarlem," and wrote the enthusiastic report that led to the founding of the city. In a small park in the heart of the metropolis, there is a monument commemorating the founder of the city, Jan van Riebeeck (1619-1677). Commissioned by the Dutch East India Company, he began to cultivate fruit and vegetables in a garden here in 1652, in order to guarantee a supply of water and vitamins on the route to India. The name of the park today, Company's Garden, recalls its origins. It is a peaceful oasis in the city, surrounded by no less than three museums: the South African Museum, the South African National Gallery and the Jewish Museum.

It said that someone who has visited Cape Town and sensed its Mediterranean flair and infectious exuberance will always be captivated by its undeniable charm. The spectacular situation, the way it nestles at the foot of Table Mountain, and above all the colorful mix of peoples in the hilly streets: all these delight the visitor. South Africa may be a Third World country, but all the comforts of western civilization are available – and this is particularly apparent in Cape Town. This cosmopolitan city has always been considered comparatively liberal. As early as 1666, one hundred Khoikhoi (Hottentots) lived in Cape Town and were generally

You can now ascend Table Mountain in one of the cabins of the cable car manufactured in Switzerland in 1997 (top), and enjoy the beautiful view to Lions Head and even to Robben Island (center). The streets in Bo-Kaap, the Malay district of Cape Town, have brightly colored houses (below).

accepted as fellow citizens. The governor, Simon van der Stel (1639–1712) ordered that slaves who had white fathers should be granted freedom. It was hardly surprising: as the son of an Indian mother, he was also a colored person himself.

Everything within the city is within easy walking distance. Fruit dealers and flower vendors peddle their goods; couples stroll along the streets; and business people eat barbecued Boer sausage. Elegant pedestrian areas with boutiques, department stores, antique shops and art galleries invite the visitor to inspect their displays. The Table Mountain massif forms the backdrop for the white city at its foot – but the mountain is often hidden by cloud and mist, its so-called "tablecloth." The most beautiful view of Cape Town and Table Mountain is to be had from Blouberg Beach, 25 kilometers (16 miles) north of the city on the ocean. In 1806 a battle took place here in which the British defeated the Dutch.

The elegant sweep of the bay of Cape Town is crowned by the glittering glass and chrome of the Victoria and Alfred Waterfront in the former harbor area. There does not seem to be enough time to see all the museums, or for rummaging at the market stalls and listening to the musicians on Green Market Square. You should also plan time for a boat trip to Robben Island, where Nelson Mandela spent 17 of his 29 years in prison as prisoner number 466/64, in cell number 5 of the high security prison. Above the entrance to the prison you can read the motto of the prison: "We Serve with Pride" – which bears an uncomfortable resemblance to the phrase that stood over the German concentration camps: "Work Brings Freedom." Those who travel with an open mind will also see the other side of the beauty – on the journey from the airport into Cape Town you will pass the slum districts. Even their optimistic names cannot disguise the hardship: Kayelitsha means "New Home" in the Xhosa language, Guguletho even means "Our Pride." Rundown shacks still testify to the former system of apartheid. The slums of corrugated iron and cardboard seem to stretch for endless distances. The dusty streets are full of trash; in the evening there is no electricity and seldom water. Nevertheless, it is apparent that in recent years a miracle has taken place in South Africa. "An unbelievable week!" was the comment of Bishop Tutu after the election and the end of the apartheid regime, and he added: "It was giddy stuff. It was like falling in love. The sky looked blue and more beautiful. I saw the people in a new light. They were beautiful, they were transfigured …"

A View of Two Oceans

Not only is the oldest city of South African a great attraction; the whole peninsula is well worth visiting. The coast on both sides has long sandy beaches, large game reserves and bird conservation areas. You can stroll along coastal promenades or relax on the beaches. One of the most beautiful coast roads in the world leads around the Cape Peninsula, offering magnificent views of the Indian Ocean and the Atlantic. Near Hout Bay, the 10-kilometer-long (6-mile) Chapman's Peak Drive covers the most spectacular section. Here, the trees for the first houses built in the Cape Colony were felled, hence the name "hout," the Dutch word for "wood." Here, too, there is a settlement where crab fishermen live. Carved in bold sweeps from the cliff face where rugged granite slopes sit on top of the red, orange and yellow colored sandstones, the coast road was considered a pioneering feat of highway engineering at the time of its construction (1915–1922). One hundred meters (328 feet) below, huge breakers crash on the jagged cliffs. Chapman's Bay owes its name to the British sailor, John Chapman, who came ashore in 1607, looking for a place to anchor and then, however, was left behind and had to struggle to survive.

The British seafarer, Sir Francis Drake, considered the promontory at the southern tip of Africa to be the most beautiful cape in the world.

In 1680, the "Flying Dutchman" sank off the Cape; this became the origin of the legend of the "Flying Dutchman" (far right). – The most popular view of Table Mountain can be photographed from Blouberg beach, north of the city (above). Colorful changing cubicles on St James beach (right).

The Cape of Good Hope Nature Reserve is not to be missed. It includes a 40-kilometer (25-mile) stretch of beach, with cliffs, flat rocks and bays with sand beaches. The road ends at a large parking area and from there one can walk to Cape Point, where the granite cliffs fall 259 meters (850 feet) into the sea. The last 40 meters (131 feet) of the trail lead over the steps up to the lighthouse high above the ocean. From here there is a view to the Cape of Good Hope itself, where banks of seaweed sparkle like black diamonds in the turquoise ocean. On the east coast of the peninsula between the Cape and Cape Town, Simon's Town lies at the foot of a 678-meter-high (2,224 feet) mountain ridge. Named after Governor Simon van der Stel, the town was chosen by the Dutch East India Company in 1741 as a winter harbor. The townscape is characterized by narrow lanes, old-fashioned pubs and the "historic mile" with its cultural sights, especially the attractive cottages. On busy Jubilee Square, directly at the water's edge, stands a bronze statue of "Just Nuisance," a Great Dane which

was a mascot for the British Navy during the Second World War. However, the town has another surprise in store. Penguins have also settled here, African (or Jackass) penguins that waddle with dignity along the beach. Leave time to visit the National Botanical Gardens of Kirstenbosch at Rhodes Drive, with their many exotic and indigenous plants.

Peaceful Small Towns in the Wine Country

The region around Cape Town is famous for its many winegrowing estates where guests can participate in wine-tasting events. They lie in the shadow of high mountains: small, peaceful little towns with old cottages, thatched roofs, small-paned windows, stucco gables, lace curtains and ornamented verandas. In the front gardens, roses and lilac bushes flourish; in the courtyards behind the houses there are cafes and art galleries, and beneath poplar and cedar trees even

Emily Hobhouse – Helping in a British Concentration Camp

Emily Hobhouse was born on April 9, 1860 in the village of St Ives near Liskeard (Cornwall) in England. She cared self-sacrificingly for 120,000 Boer women and children who had been imprisoned in the internment camps of the British Army in Bloemfontein, Kroonstad, Norvalspont, Aliwal North, Springfontein, Potchefstroom, Kimberley, Oranje River and Mafeking, and brought their plight to the attention of the British government. The British peer, Lord Roberts, had these people interned in camps during the second Boer War (1899–1902) because the women had supplied their soldiers with food. A total of 26,370 women and children died from hunger and disease in the camps. In October 1900, Emily Hobhouse founded the "Relief Fund for South African Women and Children." She later received financial support that enabled her to purchase a house in Cornwall where she spent her last years. She died on June 8, 1926. Her ashes were buried at the foot of the Women's Memorial in Bloemfontein.

the corrugated iron huts of the black migrant workers seem almost picturesque. Here you will find all facets of a "rainbow nation of the whites" – Boers (Dutch), English, French, but scarcely any black people. The luxurious lodgings in old renovated buildings in the

From the Cape of Good Hope, you can look down on the thundering waves breaking in the sunlight (large photo and right). – With a little luck, you may even see whales (top). The beautiful beaches at Clifton, a suburb of Cape Town, are very popular because the granite cliffs and rock formations provide shelter from the unpleasant southeast trade wind (above).

wine region of the Cape, in the shade of flame trees, jacarandas and palm-like cycads, set amidst a sea of blossoms of hibiscus, blood lilies and azaleas, have an unmistakably European character. They are built in the Georgian, Victorian or Cape Dutch style with large fireplaces, thick carpets, heavy curtains, expansive sofas and gold wallpaper. On the walls hang etchings of fox hunts and London mail coaches; classical music is played at dinner; and then, when an attentive (still, of course, black-skinned) waiter serves a glass of port on a silver tray, you could almost believe that the British-Boer Union of South Africa had never ended.

The history of South African wine is inseparable from the history of the region. Even in the 17th century, Jan van Riebeeck had the idea of growing wine in the Company's Gardens in Cape Town. But the location of his vineyard was poorly chosen, because the winds

from the Cape were often bitterly cold. Later, his successor, Simon van der Stel, who knew more about winegrowing, decided to move the vines from the Company's Gardens to his farm estate Groot Constantia, south of Cape Town, where they flourished. In 1679, accompanied by winegrowers from the Rhineland and France, he settled in a fertile valley near the Cape Peninsula. Nestled in this hilly landscape are many houses in the Cape Dutch Baroque style. One of the first wines of the region, a Muscadet from Groot Constantia, even surpassed the French wines. The townscape of Stellenbosch demonstrates how successful the wine business became. After Cape Town, it was the earliest white settlement in South Africa, founded in 1679 in a wide valley surrounded by mountains. The place where Governor Simon van der Stel had camped during his inspection of the country was later called "van der Stel's bush" – Stellenbosch.

In spring, the landscape is transformed by the fruit trees in the gardens into a mass of blossoms, while the slopes of the mountains are covered with vines. Stellenbosch is the most romantic town in South Africa, with long oak-lined avenues, parks and Victorian and Georgian, but mainly Cape Dutch architecture. The entire heart of the old town is a settlement of these white houses with their curved front gables. The picturesque streets are lined by oak trees planted by van der Stel in the 17th century, giving rise to the name Town of Oaks. In the course of the years, the town has become the center of the winegrowing area on the Cape. Romantic wine routes lead in all directions. When the vine leaves change color in the fall, it is impossible to escape the charm of the landscape. Indeed, if it were not for the cobras and puff adders in the vineyards, one could almost forget that this is Africa.

See page 52

Cape Dutch architecture near "Old Drostdy" in Swellendam.

A Diversity of Building Styles

Cape Architecture

1

3

2

*In many places the splendid Cape Dutch architecture reflects the prosperity of the wine estates, as in Boschendal, one of the oldest wineries (2), or in Franschhoek, a Huguenot settlement (3). – Victorian architecture, of which there are fine examples in Grahamstown (1) and in the South African Museum in Cape Town, (4) was very different.
5 In contrast – the ultra-modern smoked glass facade of the "Cape Sun Hotel" in Cape Town.*

The simple and yet elegant Cape Dutch style is probably the most typical architectural style on the Cape. It developed between the 17th and 19th centuries. The square farmhouses consist of a framework of beams, filled out with straw and clay. Characteristic features include the steep thatched roof, symmetrically arranged windows and wooden shutters. Only the lower half of the small-paned sliding windows can be opened. The dwelling house, stables, barn and servant's accommodation form a rectangular farmstead around an inner courtyard. The buildings are normally painted white and decorated with green trim. In front of the main entrance there is a flight of steps made of bricks (Dutch: *stoep*). With increasing prosperity, the houses were enlarged, a veranda was added and the front section of the house now contained a living room (voorkamer – front room) and – separated by a richly decorated wooden screen – a second room (agterkamer), usually an office or a workroom. From these centrally placed rooms, doors opened into the other rooms, such as bedrooms and kitchen. Another distinctive feature of the Cape Dutch style is the curved gables which were already fashionable in Holland in

the 17th and 18th centuries. The end gable served to prevent the roof being torn off in a storm, and the central gable provided light for the attic. The front door was made in the style of a stable door, and above it were decorations in the form of carvings, ornaments and figures. Frequently, the name or coat of arms of the family and the date when the house was built were displayed here.

By the end of the 18th century it had already become customary no longer to construct country homes on a square ground plan around an inner courtyard, but to build a two-story house in the style of the Georgian townhouses with a triangular ornamental gable and a less steeply pitched roof. The facades were adorned with additional features such as pillars and garlands and usually painted in pastel colors. The ceilings and walls inside the houses were adorned with trompe-l'oeil paintings. This architectural style is frequently found in the Malay district of Cape Town, but also became a model for many of the typical small Karoo country houses. Other examples can still be seen in Grahamstown, with the typical sliding divided-light windows, front gables and a fanlight. Slatted shutters on the windows subdue the sunlight. In the middle of the 19th century, the Gothic Revival style influenced Cape architecture, especially with regard to church architecture, the most influential architect being Sir Herbert Baker (1862–1946). Houses built later in the Victorian and Edwardian styles reflect the British influence in the 19th and 20th centuries. Typical of the Victorian style is that many dwelling houses had steep, pointed roofs and highly elaborate wrought iron decoration, brass fittings and leaded windows, as well as ornate iron verandas that were protected by corrugated iron roofs. The wrought iron ornamentation is known as broekie lace because it resembles the lace underwear that ladies wore.

An Excursion to the "French Corner"

As early as 1688, French Huguenots settled in the valley north of Stellenbosch. This region then became known as Franschhoek, the "French Corner." The settlers were 150 families who had fled to South Africa to escape the henchmen of Louis XIV. They had immediately begun to plant wines on the slopes of the Hex Mountains. The devastating infestation with phylloxera that also affected South Africa in the 19th century reached Franschhoek later than other areas and was not quite as disastrous as for the other winegrowers further south. It was decided to keep taking grafts of the French vines until they had adapted to the conditions of the region, which can be quite harsh at times. The vintners imported vines from France and from then on grew resistant Chardonnay, Pinot Noir or Merlot grapes.

At the town boundary of Franschhoek stands the Huguenot Memorial, a granite monument erected in 1938 in memory of their expulsion from their European homeland. In a park, a semicircular columned walk forms an amphitheatre with three tall arches. They represent the Trinity and rise up behind the figure of a woman who is enthroned on a globe and holds a Bible in her right hand. The broken chain symbolizes the successful liberation from religious oppression. The nearby museum is dedicated to the troubled history of the Huguenots. In the Huguenot Memorial Museum, a copy of the Edict of Nantes (1598) may be seen, the document that guaranteed Protestants in France the freedom to practice their religion.

European Traditions along the "Wine Route"

It is impossible to think of the words "wine route" without immediately thinking of the Paarl Wine Route with its magnificent landscape of wide valleys framed by strange rock formations. Some of the most attractive winegrowing estates of South Africa are to be found here. In 1687, Dutch colonists were granted their own farmland in the beautiful Berg River Valley at Perlenberg (Peerlbergh). In contrast to Franschhoek, Paarl is still a strictly conservative region – a legacy of those Boers who settled here and created their own artificial language from a Dutch dialect. Here the Bible was first translated into Afrikaans and on the slopes above the town, the Afrikaans Language Monument (Taal Monument) seems to point like a finger, saying: "Do not forget our roots!" The imposing monument consists of three domes, three small columns of different heights, an obelisk and a tall pillar that represent the meager influence of each culture. The town was founded in 1717 and its name is derived from the large protruding granite rock formation nearby that in a certain light gleams like a pearl. The elegant, white mansions sit at the end of symmetrical avenues of oak trees; the wineries are situated in old shady parks. Today Paarl is still regarded as one of the world centers of brandy culture. Not far away is the Boschendal Wine Estate (Groot Drakenstein), a farm dating from the year 1855 and one of the best examples of

Because of its sheltered location, Simon's Town was once used as the winter harbor for Cape Town and a British naval base (top). – The streets of this little coastal town feature old-fashioned pubs and the "historical mile" with its attractive houses (bottom). Approximately 4,000 varieties of plants can be seen in the Kirstenbosch National Botanical Gardens (right-hand page).

Cape Dutch farm architecture. It is not only one of the oldest wine estates of South Africa, but also one of the most important for red wines. Surrounding the farmhouse there are old pine and oak trees. The restaurant serves genuine French gourmet food and excellent wines. The museum has an exhibition of exquisite furniture and porcelain from the Dutch East India Trading Company.

The Stifling Atmosphere of Apartheid has Vanished

At first glance, the splendid Victorian facades in Swellendam seem to say that time has stood still. The town was founded in 1745 by Dutch settlers, the third white settlement after Cape Town and Stellenbosch, and was named after the Governor Hendrik Swellengrebel and his wife Helena ten Damme. The old oak-lined avenues and many historical buildings make the town well worth visiting – the old magistrate's residence (Old Drostdy), for example. The British-Boer mentality of the whites who live here has now been replaced by the vibrant rhythm of the new beginning without the oppressiveness of apartheid.

It is not far to the coast, along a route through a hilly landscape of fields and meadows. Charming little towns can be found on this stretch of coastline, such as Hermanus, a retirement location and well-known resort for whale watching; Kleinmond (also known as Proteadorp), a popular vacation resort; or Bredasdorp, named after Michiel van Breda, a sheep breeder and the first mayor. When the town was founded in 1838, there was such an argument between the farmers regarding the site of the first church, that some of them began their own building right away. The others erected their own church a short distance away, and around this the small town of Napier gradually grew up. Not far away is Waenhuiskrans, which derives its name from a cave in the cliffs that is so big that an ox-drawn wagon could turn around in it. The town, sometimes also known as Arniston (because of a troop transport ship that sank off the coast in 1815), has a long sand beach bordering the turquoise ocean. Finally, we reach Cape Agulhas (Needle Cape), the rocky promontory that forms the southernmost tip of Africa, where the Indian and Atlantic oceans merge. While the Atlantic and the ice-cold Benguela current have created an infertile desert on the west coast of South Africa, the Indian Ocean with its warm Agulhas current gives rise to lush subtropical vegetation on the east coast. The Cape itself is not very spectacular. The lighthouse, in which a museum is located, was modeled on the lighthouse at Alexandria in Egypt, and is not only the second oldest in the country, but also the most southerly in Africa. Beyond the horizon lies the Antarctic. The mix of Atlantic and Indian Ocean gives rise to dangerous currents in which many ships met their doom. Numerous wrecks testify to this. They were stranded on the rocky needles to which the Cape owes its name – "agulhas" means needle in Portuguese.

The wine estate at Boschendal is more than 300 years old and features a picnic meadow and a wine sales booth. It is surrounded by beautiful old trees (left-hand page). – The Huguenot Memorial at Franschhoek symbolizes the freedom of religion. The female figure is holding a broken chain in her left hand and a Bible in her right (above). – In Piet Retief, named for one of the leaders of the Boers, there are mineral springs; this is a picture of the church (left).

The gloriette in the park of Boschendal Wine Estate.

Fine Vintages

The Wines of South Africa

1 Coat of arms of the Neetlingshof Wine Estate, founded by German vintners. – 2 The Bergkelder Wine Estate in Stellenbosch. – 3 Rheboksloof Wine Estate – Because of its mild climate, good soils and year-round precipitation, southwest Cape Province is particularly suited to the cultivation of fruit, vegetables and wine, as these pictures of the vineyards at Rheboksloof (5), the vintage at Montagu (4) and the Groot Constantia winery (6) show.

South Africa is a country which produces a remarkable range of excellent wines, as people all over the world are now in a position to discover. Only during the last three decades has wine from the Cape region really embarked on its international career – and yet it is as old as Cape Town itself, for the first governor at the Cape, Jan van Riebeeck, made the first attempts to produce wine more than three hundred years ago. It was his successor as governor, Simon van der Stel, who really succeeded. He planted vines on his farm, Groot Constantia, and also in the cliff and river landscape at Simonsberg, a good 50 kilometers (31 miles) inland and sheltered from the often bitterly cold winds at the Cape. When he died in 1712, he left eight large wine estates.

In 1688, the real wine-growing experts, around 200 French Huguenots, gathered in Paarl and Franschhoek in order to perfect their wine-growing methods in this splendid natural setting. Following the revolutionary Edict of Fontainebleau, they had fled to the Netherlands to escape from Louis XIV, who had threatened them with the death penalty for openly practicing their religion. At that time, Governor Simon van der Stel had requested the Dutch East India Company to send further colonists to the Cape region, in order to be able to supply the passing ships with food. The valley which the Huguenots settled after arriving in South Africa in this manner was named Franschhoek, and soon the soil here was producing grapes for outstanding vintage wines, champagne and cognacs.

The decisive economic expansion in wine production was experienced by the wine growers at the Cape during the war between England and France. During the continental blockade imposed in 1804, London banned all trade with France, so that South Africa, then occupied by the British, faced a hitherto unknown demand for wine, all the more so as imports from the Cape were granted tax and customs exemptions. A phylloxera epidemic at the end of the 19th century, however, almost completely

destroyed the vines. It would have been a complete disaster if the method of grafting the European noble scions onto the healthy American wild vines had not been discovered in Europe, where phylloxera had also been raging. This saved the vines of South Africa from complete destruction. By 1918 the loss in production had already been recovered.

Along the 15 wine routes north of Cape Town you can taste some 2,000 varieties of wine at 158 wine estates and cellars. A few examples of the names behind these figures are Muscat d'Alexandrie (Hanepoot), Clairette Blanche, Chenel – to mention just a few of the "noble" varieties of grape. White wines make up 60 percent of the wine growing area at the Cape. Thanks to cool winds and low nighttime temperatures, South African white wines are characterized by a fresh fruitiness and fine aroma, especially Cape Riesling, Chenin Blanc (aromatic), Colombard, Muscatel, Sémillon (good with meals), Sauvignon Blanc (fruity) and Chardonnay (rich, fruity). In the past ten years, the area cultivated for red wine has increased from 16 to 39 percent of the total. The top red wines are Cabernet Sauvignon (the most frequently grown red grape), Cinsaut, Pinotage (spicy), Cabernet Franc, Sauvignon, Gamay, Merlot (fruity, full-bodied), Pinot Noir, Tinta Barocca and Shiraz (smoky, spicy note). The quality of the wines is tested and guaranteed by a government seal on the bottle neck. But fine wines are not found only on the Cape. In the west of the country, at Olifants River and in the interior of the Little Karoo, heavy, earthy wines are harvested every year.

Plantations, Primeval Forests and Fantastic Beaches

The Garden Route

There are endless beaches at the lake region that extends eastwards from the vacation resort of Wilderness (right-hand page).

Where exactly the Garden Route begins and ends is a matter of debate. At least the 200 kilometers (125 miles) from Mossel Bay to the estuary of the Storms River at the Indian Ocean are definitely considered part of the Garden Route proper (Afrikaans: Tuinroete), but many people consider that it ends at Humansdorp near Port Elizabeth. Regardless of that, it is an El Dorado for lovers of nature and is South Africa's best-known tourist route, with numerous vacation resorts. One should not imagine the "Garden Route" simply as a road that is bordered with parks and gardens along its entire length. To be sure, one passes fruit plantations, travels past huge expanses dotted with lakes and on through other regions with fynbos and blossoming meadows. But the route also

On the way from Cape Town to the beginning of the Garden Route you can follow the romantic coastline. The faster route is to take the main highway N2. On this you pass endless wheat fields near Caledon (above) and can visit Caledon Flower Garden (right).

passes through lush tropical pine forests that sometimes extend right down to the coast, and through villages with gleaming whitewashed farmhouses in the Victorian Cape Dutch style. It also sometimes leads through densely forested areas. Here, one tree and flower reservation, state forest or bird protection area gives way to the next. There are picturesque regions with endless groves of pine and eucalyptus trees behind the flowering trees that line the roadside; along the winding roads, that sometimes cross deep gorges, there are also frequent glimpses of the ocean. In fact, the Garden Route nearly always hugs the coastline, passing kilometer-long beaches, steep rocky coast and cliffs. Besides the deserted beaches and mountain ranges with tropical forest that reach down to the coast, another surprise is the wild rivers

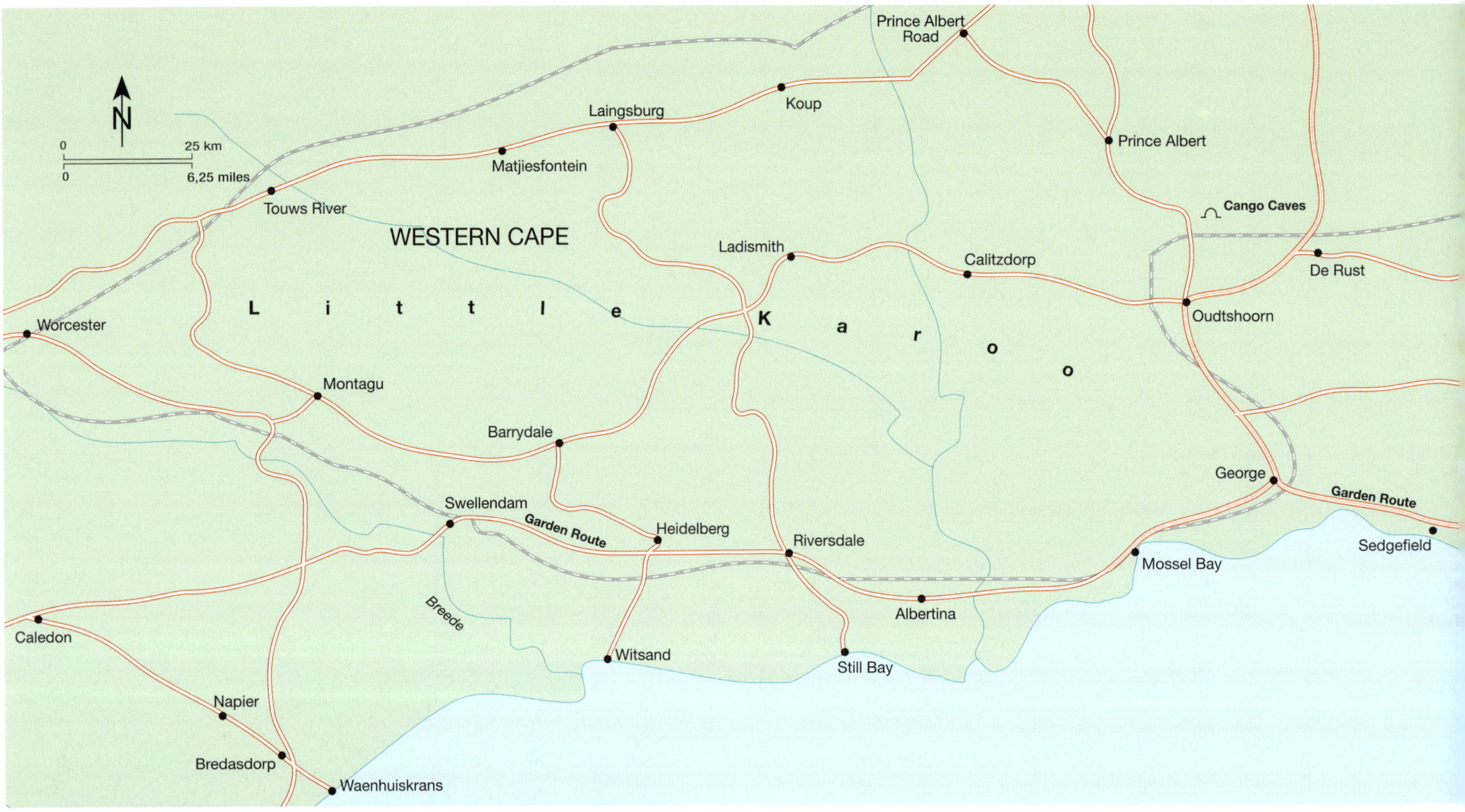

that have carved out deep canyons and formed lagoons in the lower-lying coastal areas.

Particularly between May and October it is possible to watch whales from the coast. Usually these are humpbacked and gray whales that come here from the Arctic to mate and give birth to their young in the warm waters of the Agulhas Current. At this time of year the ocean between Hermanus and Plettenberg Bay resembles a kindergarten for whales. Their magical "ocean song" penetrates into the darkest corners of the Tsitsikamma Forest.

The Garden Route and Little Karoo

The end or the beginning of the famous Garden Route, depending on whether one starts in Durban or Cape Town, is Mossel Bay ("Mussel Bay"), a vacation resort with an attractive beach for swimming. This is where Bartholomeu Dias became the first European to set foot on South African soil. On the bay, which he named after São Bras, the white settlers had their first encounter with the Khoikhoi (Hottentots). In 1596, the Dutch explorer Cornelius de Houtmann arrived in the bay and gave it the name "Mussel Bay" because of the many shells found there. In Mossel Bay there is still a 500-year-old milkwood tree known as the Post

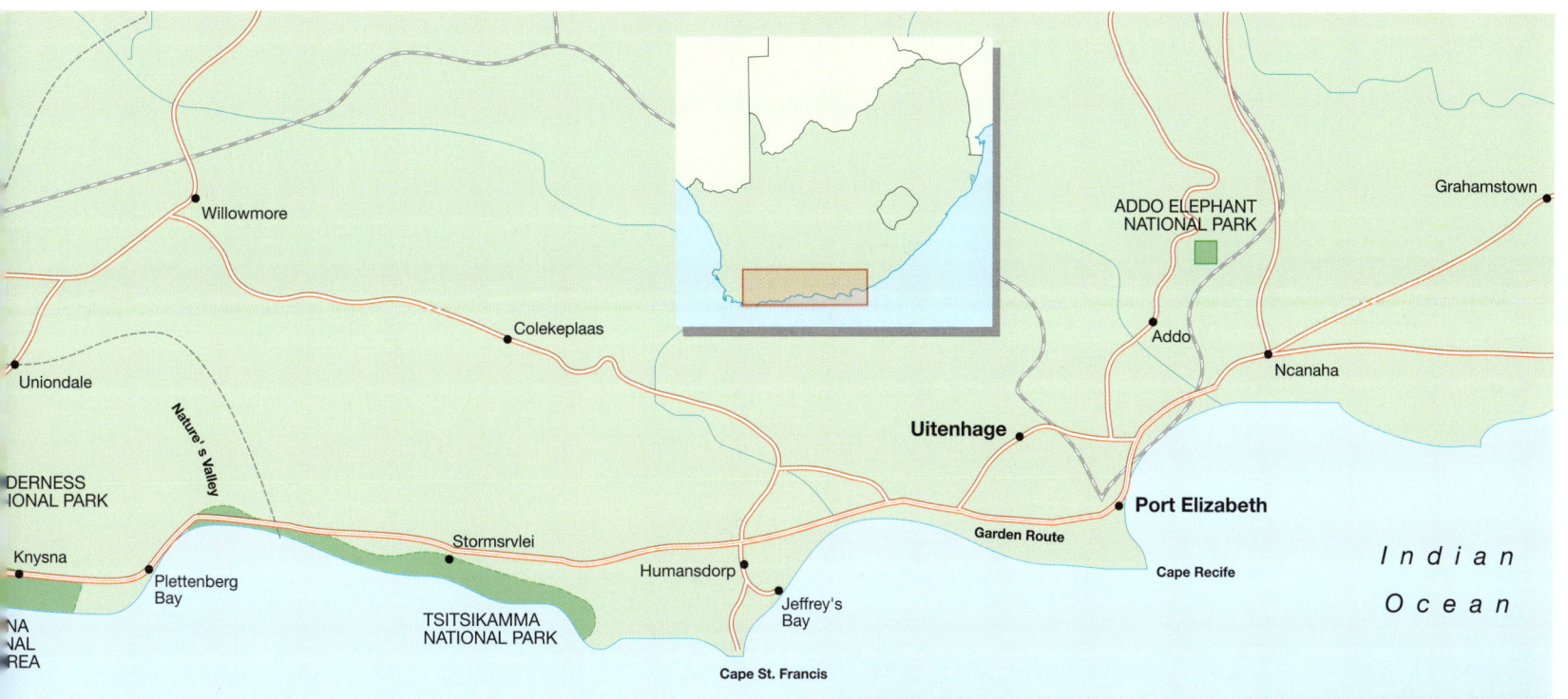

Office Tree because a seaman once left a message in a boot that he hung on the tree while on a voyage to the East Indies in 1501. The message was later found by other mariners, and this led to a custom which has been preserved until the present day. Anyone can mail a letter from the museum by posting it in the letterbox, shaped like a seaman's boot, and it will receive a special postmark. In the local Bartholomeu Dias Museum in Market Street, a replica of the caravel of the Portuguese navigator is exhibited. Beyond Mossel Bay, the Garden Route first climbs over spectacular passes into the hinterland, offering a panoramic view of the Little Karoo, a region of low vegetation. This semi-desert landscape originally consisted of semi-bush steppe and lies in the rain shadow of the mountain ranges. Because it has been over-used as pastureland, it has partly become arid semi-desert. Only at watercourses or places where groundwater can be accessed are there green flecks of color in the red-brown plateau, showing where fruit and wine are cultivated, for example, in Barrydale. The scent of the shrubs and bushes, and the light of the changing rhythm of day and year are reminiscent of the Mediterranean landscape.

From the estuary of the Kaaiman River it is only another 10 kilometers (6 miles) to George, picturesquely located at the foot of the Outeniqua Mountains on a coastal plateau, and in 1811

On the red-brown tableland of the Little Karoo there are green flecks where fruit and wine are cultivated (left-hand page), such as Barrydale (top) or Swellendam; here the Town Hall (above).

The arid Little Karoo begins beyond the Outeniqua Pass to the north of George (large photo). – Mossel Bay is a popular vacation resort with pretty buildings (right) and the famous Post Office boot (right-hand page), in which you can still post letters today.

The Outeniqua Choo-Tjoe – a Railroad Adventure

The most beautiful landscapes along the Garden Route can be experienced by taking a ride on the nostalgic, gently chugging Outeniqua Choo-Tjoe, drawn by a puffing steam engine. The narrow-gauge railroad follows the Garden Route for about 100 kilometers (63 miles) between George and Knysna and approaches the lakes of the Wilderness Area so closely that the steam from the stack of the locomotive is reflected in the water. The journey is very popular because of the dramatic panorama views across bridges, past lakes (between Wilderness and Sedgefield) and beaches (Victoria Bay) as well as through forests. High above the Kaaimans River near Wilderness, there is a breathtaking photograph opportunity when the train steams over the Kaaimans River Bridge as it crosses the deep rocky gorge. The narrow-gauge steam train departs daily from George at 8.00 a.m., except on Sundays and holidays, and arrives at approximately 10.30 a.m. in Knysna.

named after the reigning English King George III (1738–1830). The inhabitants of George describe their town as "the prettiest village and the smallest town in the world," and indeed, it is unremarkable, unless one wishes to make the journey to Knysna in the Outeniqua Choo-Tjoe train, a historical steam locomotive. There is also a large assortment of restaurants. And as the region has not only mountains and forests, but also the ocean, the entire area has become a popular choice for vacations. The world center of ostrich breeding, Oudtshoorn, is also not far away. To the north stretch the red-brown or sandy-white plains of the Great Karoo, interrupted by grey lime pans, from which in the distance occasional table mountains rise up. In the old language of the Khoikhoi, Karoo means "Place of Thirst." Indeed, it is an arid landscape with strangely formed hills in shades of yellow and brown. In this part of South Africa, isolated farmhouses, flat hilltops and rugged cliffs are the only orientation points in an otherwise empty landscape. Well worth visiting are the towns of Prince Albert, Graaf Reinet and Beaufort West, where the houses, hidden behind gardens and hedges, have richly ornamented gables, oriel windows and wooden doors. The Cango Caves, impressive stalactite caves, are also worth a detour.

Glittering Landscape – The Lake District

The lagoon basin at the Great Brak River (right, top) is one of the water landscapes with charming vacation resorts, beautiful beaches and lonely lagoons (large photo) that can be found along the Garden Route. – In the hinterland there are lush meadows for cattle and sheep. (bottom right).

To the east of George, the Garden Route suddenly takes on a very different character. The whole region between Wilderness and Knysna is known as the Lake District, because former lagoons and a series of glittering lakes (vleis), some of them interconnected, form a landscape divided from the coast by a narrow strip of dunes. Five lakes and five rivers make up the watery setting of Wilderness National Park. The Groenvlei is a freshwater lake, but the other lakes – Lower Langvlei, Upper Langvlei, Rondevlei and Swartvlei – are all salty. Between Sedgefield and Buffels Bay, to name only two of the charming vacation resorts with beautiful sand beaches, lies the Goukamma Nature Reserve, a paradise for birds.

Wilderness, one of the most popular vacation resorts, has a beautiful gold sand beach, bordered by high dunes and stretching for kilometers to the estuary of the Touw River. There is a legend that in 1877, George Bennett, a young man from Cape Town,

received permission to marry his bride only on the condition that he lived with her in the wilderness. Bennett purchased a farm, named it Wilderness and led his bride home in triumph. Today, Wilderness is one of the prettiest towns along the Garden Route and offers excellent conditions for swimming, surfing, angling and canoeing.

The "oyster town," Knysna (pronounced nyse-na) was once an industrial port for the shipment of valuable timber. In the huge lagoon at Knysna, on the widened estuary of the Knysna River, you will find crowds of anglers, divers, windsurfers and sailors. On the oceanward side, the lagoon is protected by the Heads of Knysna, two high rocky sandstone promontories, leaving only a narrow channel in the middle. One wonders nowadays how the ships managed to maneuver this channel safely. The name of this charming little town comes from the Khoikhoi word meaning "fern." It was founded by the British immigrant, George Rex who settled here in 1804. When he died in 1839, he was the largest landowner in the region. He is said to have been the son of King George III and his first wife, a Quaker, Hannah Lightfoot, who was not recognized by the court and was sent into exile after the birth of her son. In 1866 documents were discovered in the Chancery Law Court in London that some consider a valid marriage contract between Hannah Lightfoot and the Prince of Wales. One section of this controversial document states: "May, 27, 1759. This is to certify that the marriage of these parties, George, Prince of Wales, and Hannah Lightfoot was duly solemnised this day, according to the rites and ceremonies of the Church of England." The eldest of the three princes born to his marriage was George Rex.

Knysna has retained its peaceful charm and offers plenty of opportunity for shopping and strolling. An opulent meal with fish specialties can be enjoyed in the restaurant "Cranzgots," – Knysna is famous for its oysters. The fynbos-covered slopes stretch down to the beach suburb Brenton-on-Sea, to the eight kilometers (five miles) of white-sand beach and the deep blue ocean – an indescribably beautiful vista.

See page 72

The Outeniqua Choo-Tjoe steaming across the bridge over the Kaaimans River.

A Fashion Outlasting the Centuries

Ostriches – Breeding and Farms

1 A popular souvenir – a painted ostrich egg. – Wild ostriches (5) are found in South Africa, as well as the domesticated animals on ostrich farms, particularly around Oudtshoorn (4). Tourists may visit the ostrich farms, and not only purchase souvenirs, but can also ride these large flightless birds (2). Females have earth-colored plumage (3) while the male is adorned with black and white feathers (6).

What diamonds were to Kimberley, ostrich feathers were to the Little Karoo – a source of prosperity. Ostrich breeding, however, was not begun until approximately 1880. Until then, these large flightless birds were simply wild animals. The increasing demand for feathers was closely related to the beginning of the Art Nouveau period in Europe, America and Japan. The nouveau-riche "ostrich barons" invested the profits from their business in luxurious country residences which they built from sandstone in the Art Nouveau style. Within a mere ten years one of them, Max Rose, who had come to the Little Karoo from Lithuania in 1890, succeeded in gaining control of the trade in ostrich feathers. He owned an enormous farm with 10,000 birds. During World War I, the fashion for ostrich feathers ended. At the end of the 1930s, business experienced a new boom when show farms were established and began to attract tourists. Today, ostrich breeding is a well-organized business, and ostrich meat in particular is becoming increasingly popular. The hub of the ostrich breeding business is the town of Oudtshoorn, founded in 1847. The ostrich farms are located here; Highgate, Safari Ostrich and Cango Ostrich are the best known. At present there are 150 farmers in the region who own approximately 90,000 ostriches. Some ostrich farms are open to visitors; you can also purchase souvenirs and even ride the birds.

Ostriches are so heavy that in the event of danger they are unable to fly away; they have to run for their life. This they can do easily, for at more than 60 kilometers (38 miles) per hour they are the fastest two-legged creatures in the world. A flock consists of 100 to 150 birds; their feathers are plucked every nine months. Both parents take part in hatching out their eggs: the female with her earth-brown colored plumage is better adapted to the environment during the day, and the male, with his black and white feathers, at night. The growing demand for ostriches results from the fact that everything can be used: the meat is rich in vitamins and low in fat and cholesterol, fine leather can be made from the skin; and the feathers are used as a cleaning product in the IT industry or for making dusters. The exhibition "The History of the Ostrich through the Centuries" in the C. P. Nel Museum at Oudtshoorn displays information about ostrich breeding, and about this flightless bird.

71

Bathing Beaches and Fairytale Forests

Situated on a wide sweeping bay, Plettenberg Bay also has attractive beaches for swimming and lagoons sheltered from the wind. The town is enthroned on red sandstone cliffs that rise above the 12-kilometer-long (8-mile) beach and the lagoon that was formed by the Keurbooms and Bietou Rivers. Given the name Bahia Formosa (Beautiful Bay) by the Portuguese seafarer Manuel de Pesetrello in 1577, the town owes its present name to the Governor Baron Joachim van Plettenberg (born in Holland in 1739), who took possession of the bay in 1799 for the Dutch East India Company. Vacation and retirement homes cling to the slopes, built close together, so that from a distance the town looks like a walled medieval city. This delightful region has remained the domain of the whites. "Plett," as the South Africans refer to it, is the "Saint-Tropez of South Africa" and that is reflected in the prices.

From Plettenberg Bay to Tsitsikamma National Park you must take either the toll highway N2 leading through the forests and the high coastal plains, or – the better choice – the delightful R102, winding through the 183-meter-deep (600-foot) gorge of the Bloukrans River. The name Tsitsikamma (Place of Many Waters) is derived from a Khoikhoi word. This is a fascinating forest with more than 100 varieties of tree, including beautiful timber such as stinkwood (alder) and yellowwood. The 200-year-old stinkwood trees got their name from the unpleasant smell of the freshly cut wood. In this fairytale, primeval forest, other varieties such as redwood (ironwood), candle wood (wild olive) and Cape ash trees also flourish. Hiking trails lead through a jungle of ferns, moss, climbing plants and shrubs. In Tsitsikamma Forest you could almost imagine that you have been set down in the world of John Ronald Reuel Tolkien. The idea is not so far-fetched: it was here that the author, who was born on January 3, 1892 in Bloemfontein, found inspiration for his fantasy epic "Lord of the Rings."

Beyond the 190-meter-long (207-yard) Paul Sauer Bridge with its view towards the mountains and down into the gorge, a side road leads to the park entrance of Tsitsikamma Coastal National Park, stretching for many kilometers with breathtaking panoramas between Groot River Mouth and Plettenberg Bay. At the low-lying sections of the coastline there are beautiful lagoons. Nature's Valley, for example, is surrounded by rainforest and mangrove swamps. Heather and proteas grow all along the steep

*The attractive resort of Buffel's Bay is well known for its beaches which extend to Brenton-on-Sea (large photo).
– From the Paul Sauer Bridge there is an impressive view into the Canyon of the Storms River (left).
– Knysna is a romantic little town on the Garden Route, with specialty restaurants; here, the old Saint George's Church (below).*

coast. Orchids, heather and lilies bloom along the banks and pools. The white sand beach and the picture-book lagoon at the mouth of the Groot River Delta are framed by a backdrop of cloud-covered mountains. This landscape is addictive.

Beyond the romantic little town of Humansdorp, the road winds through flat, green land with fenced-in pastureland, sheep and cattle, so that Ireland immediately springs to mind. It is only 12 kilometers (8 miles) to St Frances Bay, a mecca of the rich, where the vacation villas have thatched roofs. Blacks are welcome here only in the role of domestic servants. The whites reside in a luxurious ghetto, far removed from the social reality in South Africa. You can find a place to stay here or in Jeffrey's Bay if you do not want to stay in the permanently overcrowded town of Port Elizabeth, although the latter offers many distractions.

The "Detroit of South Africa"

Beyond the Garden Route lies Port Elizabeth, the industrial center and port often referred to as the "Detroit of South Africa." Once loyally British and bound by the old traditions, this is now an open-minded city with numerous bars, restaurants and enter-

The sophisticated "Island Hotel" is surrounded by magnificent sand beaches at Plettenberg Bay (top). At Jeffrey's Bay there are good conditions for surfers and windsurfers (above). – Port Elizabeth has developed into a modern center for entertainment. This shows the Roman Catholic Church (right). – Right-hand page: In Addo Elephant National Park you can enjoy good views of the animals when they gather at waterholes, attack each other or compete to test their strength.

tainment centers. The city lies on the west coast of Algoa Bay. It was founded in 1820 by British settlers. The heart of the city is Market Square, where the City Hall was modernized after a fire in 1977; it is now an historic monument. In front of the City Hall there is a replica of the cross that Bartholomeu Dias erected in 1488 when he first came ashore at Algoa Bay. The King's Fountain on Market Square commemorates the coronation of Queen Elizabeth II. The White House, dating from 1904, is an example of South African Art Nouveau architecture. From the 52-meter-high (170-feet) bell tower that was erected in 1923 in memory of the first settlers, there is a beautiful view over the city and the port. The Horse Memorial of 1905, depicting a soldier who is giving his horse some water, is also noteworthy. It is a memorial to the horses that were killed in the Boer War and bears the inscription: "The greatness of a nation consists not so much in the number of its people or the extent of its territory, as in the extent and justice of its compassion." In Donkin Reserve, a park on the hill, there is a pyramid to the memory of Elizabeth, the wife of Sir Rufane Donkin (1772–1841), who died in India of a fever in 1818, and a lighthouse dating from 1861. This is now an historic monument, as is the row of Victorian-era houses in Donkin Street (1860-1880). At the mouth of the Baakens river stands Fort Frederick. It was erected in 1799 by British troops, the first stone building in Eastern Cape Province.

An appropriate way to end a visit to the Garden Route is with a visit to the Addo Elephant National Park north of Port Elizabeth, between the Suurberg Range and the valley of the Sundays River. Even the earliest settlers in the Addo region began decimating the large herds of elephants, as they repeatedly destroyed their fields. The number of animals decreased until in 1919 barely a dozen remained. The Addo Elephant National Park was set up in 1931 for their protection. Today more than 200 elephants inhabit the park, along with buffalo and a number of varieties of antelope.

Storms River Mouth: a view of the raging ocean.

An Expression of Tribal Identity

The Art of the Ndebele

1 Magnificently adorned Ndebele woman in Botshabelo Village. – The colorful houses and garden gates (2) with expansive geometrical patterns (6) are miniature works of art. – 3 Ndebele women are happy to pose for a photo in front of their artistically decorated buildings. – Splendid examples of Ndebele art can also be seen at Kwandebele (4) and Loopspruit (5) near Pretoria.

Known as Matebele in the rest of southern Africa, the Ndebele are members of the Nguni family of the Bantu, along with the Xhosa, Swazi and Zulu peoples. They moved to the southernmost part of the continent during the great migration of the African peoples in the 16th century. In the 19th century they were forced by the expansion of the Zulus to withdraw again to the north. A small remainder stayed in a South African enclave in what was then Transvaal. They finally were forced to capitulate in 1893 following bloody conflicts under King Nyabela (condemned to death on September 22, 1883, with the sentence later commuted to life imprisonment) with the leader of the Boers, Piet Joubert (1882/83), and under King Lobengula (1833–1984) with Cecil Rhodes. The female members of the tribe wear hoops and stiff beaded work that designate certain periods of their life. The neck is adorned with brass hoops extending up to the chin; it becomes elongated with the years as new hoops are added. Brass hoops and beaded bracelets also adorn their arms and legs. Sometimes the women even wear copper hoops around the hips. In addition, they wear heavy bands of woven grass or animal hair, with colored beads that used to be made of mud and goats milk. The children also adorn their throats, but only with woven straw. The rows of beads and the beaded embroidery of the younger girls are different from the beaded jewelry of the women and of the girls who are undergoing their initiation ceremony to prepare them for their life as women. The patterns used are also found on household implements and weapons and on the woven fabrics for carpets and cloaks.

The Ndebele could only develop the art of wall painting after the people became settled, as nomads normally do not paint their walls. The century-long development of the patterns for the beaded embroidery also found application in the murals. The women applied

a mixture of cow dung and clay on the walls, and – as soon as the clay had dried – began drawing fine lines in the damp surface using their fingertips. They used earth dyes which often had to be brought from long distances. They knew where to find the dark black *uthamboti* of a scented wood, the red clay *isibomvu* and the ocher *usomashwabada* from river sand or *uswayi* white. Today they buy acrylic paint which they mix with clay to achieve the traditional pastel shades. The colors have symbolic meanings: pink refers to poverty, red means tears, yellow is for riches and green for jealousy.

The murals on the houses feature linear, geometrical components. Corresponding to the beading technique, horizontal, vertical and diagonal lines are drawn on the walls. The black lines drawn on a white ground resemble print characters and are known as *amagama*.

Visitors who are interested in traditional African culture and lifestyle can visit Botshabelo Village north of Middleburg or the Ndebele village, Loopspruit, north of Pretoria, where the development of Ndebele architectural styles through the centuries has been documented. Small items of jewelry and fabrics can also be purchased there.

Corridors of Rock and the "Dragon's Ridge"

Land of Xhosa und Zulu

The entire coastal region between Port Elizabeth and Durban has the reputation of being one vast, continuous beach for visitors in search of relaxation. And indeed, the water of the Indian Ocean here is warm all year round, and the beaches are endless. Hidden lagoons attract swimmers, rocky cliffs alternate with gentle green hills, and small bays with magnificent sand beaches with mangrove swamps. The hinterland, with its Xhosa settlements, is no less diverse than the splendid coastal region.

Settler's Country – a Little Piece of England in the Land of the Xhosa

From the end of the Garden Route near Humansdorp to the Great Kei River northeast of East London lies a region that has acquired the name Settler's Country, because many immigrants settled here at the beginning of the 19th century. This area, including Jeffrey's Bay, Port Elizabeth, Grahamstown, King William's Town and East London, had already been settled by the Boers in the 18th century. They found rich pastures for their herds, and this very quickly led to hostile confrontations with the Xhosa who already lived there. The round huts (rondavels) of the Xhosa with their cone-shaped grass roofs are normally built of stone, but sometimes also with clay bricks. The huts are painted blue and the door always faces east, in order to protect the inhabitants from evil spirits. Occasionally one still sees older Xhosa women with their typical,

The Qwaqwa Mountains (top) and the Royal Natal National Park (right-hand page) are a paradise for nature lovers. – A Xhosa woman selling pineapples (above).

orange colored robes, turban-like headdresses and a long pipe, the status symbol of married women.

Grahamstown, named after its founder, Colonel John Graham (1778–1821), is a city with modern, outward-looking flair. This is not least because of the influence of the students who live here in order to study at the prestigious Rhodes University. There are more than 40 churches and neat and tidy Victorian and Georgian houses, as if a piece of England had been transplanted to Africa. And yet it is located right in the center of the Xhosa tribal lands, and was for a long time used as a military post. Consequently, Gunfire Hill rises above the town along with the star-shaped Fort Selwyn and the Settler's Monument in memory of the settlers from 1820. In contrast, the monotonous rows of small matchbox-like brick houses in the residential district of the blacks seem very dreary. They are slum districts constructed from corrugated iron and salvaged pieces of wood. Between Grahamstown and East London, the green landscape is reminiscent of Ireland. Morning mist hangs over the road and salty air wafts in from the ocean. East London, situated at the estuary of the Buffalo River, is

Immaculate Victorian buildings form the center of Grahamstown (above). – Xhosa women in this university city (top). – Bunga ("Talking Shop") is the name of the parliament in Umtata (right-hand page, bottom).
In Idutywa there is a colorful Xhosa market (right). – The Kei River marked the border between the Transkei and the Ciskei (right-hand page, top).

the only river port of South Africa and is hemmed in between the former borders of Transkei in the east and Ciskei in the west. Today the entire urban area is known as Buffalo City. The city center extends on both sides of the wide Main Street with its jewel of a City Hall in the Victorian Renaissance style from the year 1897. The bell tower is dedicated to Queen Victoria, and an equestrian memorial in front of City Hall commemorates the whites who fell in the Boer War. On the southern bank of the Buffalo River still stand the remains of the old Glanmorgan fortress that once formed part of a chain of forts erected against the Xhosa. There is also a German Settler's Memorial specifically commemorating the German settlers who arrived in 1857.

Cliffs and Lonely Bays – The Wild Coast

The long, rocky and picturesque coastal strip between the Great Kei River, northeast of East London, and the Umtamvuna River at Port Edward is not without reason known as the Wild Coast. Unbridled and ferocious, the ocean breaks on the coastline and has hammered out huge tunnels and craters in the defiant cliffs. One of the greatest challenges for seafarers of earlier times on the East Asia Route was to master these tricky conditions despite the storms, submerged rocks and unpredictable currents. Some ships just disappeared; others were shattered on the rocks. Chests full of gold are said to have been lost then, and even a Persian throne. Entire "shipwreck routes" have developed along the coast – a paradise for divers. On this storm-lashed coast, there are rocks that erosion has shaped like buildings created by human hands. Cathedral Rock rises up amidst raging waters, only a few meters from the coast. Further south, an island off Coffee Bay resembles the back of a whale. Here, where the island has been breached in the middle by the relentless assault of the ocean and the Mpako River, the wind often whistles through a hole in the rocks and seems to sing a song. The Xhosa named this natural opening in the rocks through which the waves break, Esikhaleni (Place of Noise). The rather more prosaic Europeans called it "Hole in the Wall." It is testimony to a tragic chapter in the history of the Xhosa. In 1856, a Xhosa girl called Nongquawuse received inspiration that the spirits of dead Xhosa warriors would come through the Hole in the Wall to drive all the white people back into the ocean, if all the

The diverse landscape of Xhosa country has steep valleys and rivers carrying plenty of water, as well as grasslands on the slopes of the mountains (large photo). – Clock tower of the City Hall in East London (right).

cattle were killed and the fields burnt down. The Council of the Elders believed the young woman. After massacring 30,000 head of cattle, the Xhosa died in misery from hunger. The British then closed the mission stations, but the subsequent famine took the lives of about 25,000 people.

From Port Edward, the most northeasterly point of the Wild Coast, the route continues along the South Coast, divided into the Hibiscus Coast in the south and the Sunshine Coast in the north, as far as Amanzimtoti. The name is derived from an exclamation of the Zulu king, Shaka, when he drank the refreshing water of the river: "Amanzi umtoti" (the water is sweet). The coastline is dotted with resorts, all with excellent, partly rocky beaches. In between there are sandy bays with comfortable hotels, camp sites and vacation resorts.

Extravagantly costumed rickshaw driver in Durban (left). – The City Hall of Durban also houses the Natural Science Museum (right).

Boomtown Durban

After such unadulterated experiences of nature, the arrival in Durban may at first seem like a shock. When Vasco da Gama, the Portuguese explorer, first reached the new land on the Indian Ocean at the bay near Durban on Christmas Eve 1497, he called the river that flowed into the ocean here the Rio da Natal (River of the Birth) and the land Terra Natalis. This gave its name to the present-day province of Natal. The missionary Allen Francis Gardiner (1794–1851) then named the original trading post dating from 1835 after the governor of the Cape Colony at that time, Sir Benjamin d'Urban (1777–1849), which then became Durban. It is a busy and exuberant commercial metropolis. And as a special achievement, it has simultaneously managed to become estab-

The Howick Falls cascade into a gorge near Pietermaritzburg (right). The most spectacular part of the Royal Natal National Park is the "Amphitheater" in the south of the park (large photo). Bushman drawings can be seen in Giants Castle National Park (right-hand page).

lished as a vacation center. Apart from possessing the second-largest port in Africa, Durban, was originally given the label "exotic," for the third largest city in Africa is also the center of a large Indian community. It was during a train journey from Durban to Pretoria, by the way, that a young Indian lawyer was thrown out of the first-class compartment onto the platform at Pietermaritzburg, as first class was reserved exclusively for the use of whites. His name was Mahatma Gandhi (1896–1948).

The visitor to Durban will note a certain similarity with Florida. This city "where the fun never ends" (according to one advertising slogan) reveals its outward-looking and tourist-oriented aspect most clearly on the six-kilometer-long (four-mile) Golden Mile, where luxury hotels, exclusive restaurants, discos, bars, nightclubs, fun parks and sales booths are clustered. Windsurfers glide elegantly over the waves and joggers trot along the beach front. The marina is crowded with elegant yachts. Near the aquarium, one sees the much-photographed rickshaw drivers with their colorful costumes and fantastic headdresses, as well as the lavishly-decorated two-wheeled rickshaws.

The "Dragon's Ridge" – The Drakensberg

The Drakensberg, the second-highest mountain range in Africa after the Kilimanjaro Massif, stretches for more than one thousand kilometers (625 miles) from the northeast of Mpumulunga Province to the Kingdom of Lesotho, forming the easternmost and most scenic region of the great African escarpment. Separated by a depression, the two sections of the range are known as the Northern Transvaal Drakensberg, with the Panorama Route, and the Natal Drakensberg. The name was given by the Boer Trekkers, because the peaks reminded them of the back of a dragon. In the Zulu language, the mountains are called Qathlamba (Barrier of Spears) because of the jagged ridge. The somber, rugged wall of Cathkin Peak near Giants Castle, broken up by innumerable rivers and bridges, forms a section of the Giant's Castle Game Reserve and is one of the most impressive sections of the Drakensberg. The region is overshadowed by a 3,000-meter-high (9,842-foot) basalt wall. The game reserve lies on a grassy plateau and was created in 1904 to protect the large eland antelope. It consists of a high plateau with valleys and mountain slopes that gradually give way to the rugged basalt face of the Drakensberg. In the caves in the mountains, cave paintings of the San (Bushmen) depicting hunting scenes and shamanic rituals and testifying to the cultural life of the oldest people in southern Africa have been discovered: in the Main Caves alone, 500 paintings can be admired. At the end

of 2002, a rock overhang was discovered on which more than five thousand of these drawings can be seen.

In the south of Royal Natal National Park, the most spectacular section of the Drakensberg, the imposing "Amphitheater" rises like a majestic cliff face, an 8-kilometer-long (5-mile) crescent-shaped section of the Great Escarpment, framed by the twin peaks Sentinel and Eastern Buttress. As there are no foothills here, this high basalt wall rises steeply from its base to 1,800 meters (5,905 feet) in height. Points, towers, pillars and columns and, in between, deep gorges are evidence of the mighty power of erosion. The high plateau is overshadowed in the background by the 3,282-meter-high (10,768-foot) Mont-aux-Sources that was named "mountain of springs," by the two French missionaries who were the first whites to climb it in the 1930s. The mountain is a watershed for the Oranje River flowing west and the Tugela River flowing east, for the first two kilometers over cascades and

See page 92

Royal Natal National Park is the watershed of South Africa, with the Oranje River flowing towards the Atlantic and the Tugela River towards the Indian Ocean. This beautiful park can be explored on numerous hiking trails.

The "Switzerland of Africa"

The Kingdom of Lesotho

The Sani Pass (3) is a spectacular pass through the mountains that is approached from the Umkomanazana River Valley (2) coming from KwaZulu-Natal. – In Lesotho, one still sees yoked oxen working the fields (1). – Young woman during her initiation ritual (4).

The immediate impression is of a wide-screen movie set in Mongolia, with wild horsemen, lonely mountains and an expansive mountainous region. But this is a movie about Africa, and the country is called Lesotho. In winter, snow regularly blankets the highlands (highveld), where the peaks can reach heights of up to 3,000 meters (9,843 feet). Like an island within the territory of South Africa lies the land that is known as the "Switzerland of Africa" or the "Roof of Southern Africa." This small state, which likes to call itself the "Kingdom of Heaven," is proud of the fact that its inhabitants, the Basotho, have never been expelled from the "Mountain of Darkness." The first inhabitants of present-day Lesotho are considered to be the San (Bushmen), of whom the numerous rock and cave drawings serve as a reminder. It is possible to see some just before reaching Nazareth by taking the small track which turns left towards the village of Ha Khotso. From there it is a five-kilometer (3-mile) hike to the Ha Baroana Rock Paintings (Place of the Little Bushman).

The San were later displaced by the Nguni tribes, who entered the region through the passes across the Drakensberg from Natal and settled along the Caledon River. From 1820 onwards, the Sotho joined them, a fairly small tribe of the Bantu family that withdrew in 1824 to a natural fortress to escape from the remaining Zulu under King Shaka, who were fleeing from the Dutch settlers. This became

4

known as Thaba Bosiu (Mountain of Darkness) because they first reached it at night; today it is called Maseru. During the fourth decade of the 19th century, the Sotho faced another threat, for the Great Boer Trek was now proceeding into the regions north of the Oranje River. Nonetheless, until his death in 1870 the Sotho Chief Moshoeshoe I succeeded in playing off against each other the Boers and the British government at the Cape. In the face of bitter opposition from the Boer Orange Free State, but at the request of Moshoeshoe, Basutoland became a British protectorate. On October 4, 1966 the country was granted independence. Many Basotho still work in South Africa as immigrant workers and seldom visit their home. The capital city, Maseru (meaning: Red Sandstone), was the destination of choice for visitors from South Africa during apartheid, but today it is a rather sleepy place. Founded by the British on the Caledon River in 1869, the city has not much to offer apart from the Main Street and a few unimaginative shopping centers, a cathedral showing some Romanesque influence and a few buildings from the colonial era that have little charm. But excursions to the surrounding areas are literally breathtaking and permit magnificent views of the mountain world. However, the roads in the mountains are poor, and some can only be accessed in four-wheel-drive vehicles. A unique experience for visitors is pony trekking. The Basotho pony has been repeatedly crossed over the centuries with horses that were imported to the South African Cape Province from Java, creating a race in its own right. These small but strong horses can be ridden from the Basotho Pony Trekking Centre to the Qiloane Waterfalls.

The only road from KwaZulu-Natal in South Africa to Lesotho leads over the steep, 2,874-meter-high (9,429-foot) Sani Pass. The starting point of the winding pass road is the South African hotel "Sani Pass." The journey follows the long basalt wall of the highest mountain in southern Africa, Thabana Ntlenyana (3,482 m/ 11,424 ft). One of the most beautiful mountain flowers, the suicide gladiolus, grows in its humid crevices.

"Kena ka khotso" ("Come in peace and bring peace with you") – strangers in Lesotho are greeted with these words, or possibly with: "Khotso pula naga" ("Rain, peace and prosperity"). These wishes should also be granted to this beautiful land.

then crashing over the 850-meter-high (2,789-foot) Tugela Falls into the valley. The ascent to Tiger Falls can be made from the beautifully situated Royal Natal National Park Hotel. Along the trail there is a magnificent mountain panorama in blue, red and green that may be temporarily intensified into a really dramatic atmosphere by the presence of dark clouds. The trail leads through rainforest and then on to the Gudu Falls.

Another equally splendid scenic region is the Qwaqwa Mountain range to the north of the "Amphitheater." Qwaqwa in the language of the San means "whiter than white" and refers to the color of the bleached sandstone cliffs. The vividly colored sedimentary rocks, especially slates, sandstones and mudstones, provide a stark contrast to the dark basalt in the valleys and gorges.

The Golden Gate Highlands National Park lies at the foot of the Maluti Mountains, which rise to heights of between 1,900 and 2,700 meters (6,234-8,858 feet). It is usually approached from the mountain road that leads from Bethlehem and then follows the border with Lesotho. The region around this town is called the "Siberia of South Africa", because of the exceptionally cold nights. The sandstones, colored yellow, red and orange by their iron oxide content, are flooded with golden light, especially at sunset. Two massive rock formations reaching to more than 100 meters (328 feet) in height form the "Golden Gate" through which the road leads in a series of curves. Bizarre rock formations alternate with gentle slopes, deep gorges, forests and waterfalls. The difference in elevation has shaped the unique character of this

Golden Gate Highlands National Park owes its name to the sandstone rocks that shimmer golden-yellow in the sunshine (large photo). – The Qwaqwa Mountains extend along the border with Lesotho (far left). – An aloe in bloom (left).

beautiful park. The vegetation and species of animal found here are different from those in the rest of the South African game reserves. The typical highland vegetation consists of acidic grasses and a multitude of herbs and bulbiferous plants. In the gorges, oldwood and other rare indigenous varieties of tree can be found.

Shaka – King of the Zulu

Shaka (or Chaka) was probably born in 1787 as the illegitimate son of Senzangakhona, who reigned from 1781 to 1816 and was the chief of a small Zulu tribe. He was subsequently banished with his mother, but in 1816 became the successor of Dingiswayo. Shaka ordered the conscription by force of all Zulu men. In villages set up for this purpose, so-called ekanda, the men spent two years being trained for warfare. Continual exercises were necessary, because Shaka introduced military techniques that had previously not been known to the peoples of southern Africa. Not only rival tribes, but also English contingents with modern equipment, fled more than once in panic from the Zulu warriors. On September 22, 1828, Shaka was murdered by his half-brothers Dingane and Mhlangane. On his grave in Stanger there is a memorial, and the Zulus today still revere him as the "Black Napoleon."

Natal Midlands and Valley of 1000 Hills

Between the high wall of the Drakensberg and the subtropical coastal strip lie the Natal Midlands, as the hilly plateau with its rich grasslands is known. South of Durban lie not only beautiful beaches, but also the rugged Oribi Gorge; to the north is the attractive Valley of 1000 Hills. The River Mgeni and its tributaries have carved their way through the granite and in some places are overshadowed by the growth of the red, shimmering krantz aloe, typical of South Africa. But here nothing seems threatening, as the elevations are never more than a few hundred meters. Everything is harmonious, and even natural features have pleasant names. For example, one of the hills is called Sleeping Beauty, and the Umgeni flows through the Garden

Province before flowing gently into the Indian Ocean near Durban. Here, and further to the east, is the land of the Zulu, the largest black ethnic group in South Africa. Everywhere in Durban you can admire their dances – admittedly put on for the benefit of tourists, but nevertheless still an expression of their ancient culture. The pleasant landscape of the 1000 Hills has, however, experienced a gory past. Those who wish to study the history of the conflicts between the white settlers and the black tribes will find plenty of illustrations on the battlefields. Southwest of Ulundi, markings in the ground are a reminder of Umgungundhlovu, the camp of the Zulu king Dingane, who negotiated with the Voortrekkers led by Piet Retief (1780–1838) in November 1837, but then took them prisoner in 1838, executing them and leaving them to the vultures. The reaction of Andries Wilhelmus Jacobus Pretorius (1799–1853) a rich farmer from

In the Valley of 1000 Hills, there are wide fields of sugarcane (large photo) and Zulu farmsteads (left-hand page, top). – The headdresses of married Zulu women are made of ocher and fibers with ornate beaded decoration (left).

Graaf Reinet, was to muster an army of white and mixed-race fighters. On the banks of the Tugela, not far from present-day Dundee, the situation climaxed in a massacre on December 16, 1838. The Boers, only 464 in number, formed a circle with their ox wagons. The Zulu attacked with four companies of warriors, each of which had been allotted a precisely defined task. Nonetheless, they were mown down by the cannons of the whites. After a terrible bloodbath, three thousand bodies floated in the river, giving it its infamous name of Blood River. But peace still did not come to Natal. The Boers eventually had to capitulate to the English, but the latter had their own difficulties with the Zulus, when these recovered their strength under Cetshwayo (1840–1872). They had not taken the warriors very seriously until the Zulu massacred an entire army at Isandhlwana on January 22, 1879. 1,329 soldiers were left lying on the battlefields, their stomachs slit open so that their souls could depart and not return to haunt the living. More than 1,000 Zulu warriors also met their death. On the battlefield at Rorke's Drift, in 1879, a mere 100 British soldiers held out for 12 hours against the superior force of 4,000 Zulus. The Zulus were finally defeated only one year later, in 1880, after their capital city Ulundi had been conquered.

Game Reserves and Tourism

Just two hours by car from Durban towards the northeast lies the entrance of the Hluhluwe-Umfolozi Game Reserve (pronounced "shloo-shloo-wey"). The reserve was founded in 1897 and is one of the oldest wildlife reserves in South Africa. Its name comes from the Zulu word for a climbing plant belonging to the family of butterfly flowers. White rhinoceros can be seen grazing along the roadside; thickly forested hills and the fertile valleys of the grass savanna extend towards the horizon in the background. A large herd of buffalo breaks through the high grass with tickbirds on their brown-black backs. The smell of fresh earth and the scent of plants are carried on the breeze. A largely unpaved road leads through the center of the reserve. This beautiful nature park consists of savanna, thornbush and humid montane forests. It nestles into the hills rising from the coast and provides a spacious habi-

Unmarried Zulu girls do not cover the upper part of their body (top). – Kraal PheZulu near Durban (above). – Zebras and white rhino in the Hluhluwe Game Reserve; giraffe in Phinda Game Reserve (right-hand page, from top to bottom).

tat, especially for the rare black and white rhinos. The park is also famous for the nyala, probably Africa's most beautiful and shyest species of antelope. On the mountainside, with a spectacular view of the landscape below, lies "Hilltop Camp," almost a small village, with restaurant, bar, shops and gas station. The list of species found in the park is remarkable and is set to become even more spectacular in future, when the planned corridor from the adjoining Phinda Private Game Reserve to the St Lucia Wetland Park has been completed, linking the arid region of the reserve with one of the world's unique wetland areas. The St Lucia wetland consists of the largest inland lake in South Africa, ancient coastal forests with meter-high shrubs, coral trees, white milkwood trees and wild fig trees. An ocean inlet, bordered by dense mangrove forests, connects the lake with the Indian Ocean and is an ideal habitat for leatherbacked sea turtles, hippopotamuses and flamingos. The dunes along the coast reach heights of 150 meters (492 feet). Sometimes it is even possible to see the coral gardens in the warm current from the shore. Here night is quickly chased away by day, without any romantic, glowing balls of fire on the horizon. And the night-time dew evaporates in just a few moments, and suddenly the blazing sun shines milky-yellow over the St Lucia lagoon.

The Phinda Private Game Reserve, only opened in 1992, is an area of hilly land, but also includes some flat bushland, open savanna and riverine forests. In the midst of this breathtaking natural beauty, all the large species of game and more than 350 different species of birds are found. In the language of the Zulu, Phinda means "back to nature" and, here, where seven different ecological systems from the Ubombo Mountains to the coast of the Indian Ocean adjoin one another, an incomparable paradise for animals truly exists. At the same time, Phinda is also an example for the problems which the philosophy of game reserves entails, for along its boundaries illness and poverty are rife, and the Tonga who live there have only heard of elephants and leopards, but do not see them. Their situation will become more acute, for in the north of Maputaland a mega-park is planned in which there will be no more room for the indigenous people. Visitors who stay in the exclusive lodges in the game parks such as Phinda or Itala are not confronted with the hunger and poverty of Africa. Waiters hover in dark suits, serving exquisite meat and fish dishes on the verandah. While the guest spoons his dessert, he can watch the animals coming to the water hole. The land that has had such difficulty in liberating itself from the swamp of racial hatred and political mistrust is light years away.

Zulu women and Zulu warriors at Kwa Bhekithunga.

The Kingdom of Swaziland

Ngawane

1 The Swazi kraals consist of huts that resemble beehives. – 2 Typical mountain landscape in the west of Swaziland. – 3 Curious Swazi girls at Pigg's Peak.

Visitors wishing to travel from the game reserves in KwaZulu-Natal to the Kruger National Park normally use one of the 11 border crossings for the journey through the Kingdom of Swaziland. Typical Swazi kraals with their round huts border the roadside. According to tradition, the Swazi, who derive their name from King Msawzi II, a chief of the Dlamini clan, settled between Pongolo and Great Usutu to the west of the Lebombo Mountains in the 16th century. Around 1750, they moved to Little Usutu, as they felt permanently under threat from the Zulus. Then the first white missionaries, farmers and the Boers from Transvaal began to arrive. The Swazi had an army trained for battle, but nevertheless had to concede the land north of the Crocodile River to what was then the Republic of Lydenberg in 1846. The European colonialists purchased land, mining and trade concession rights from King Mbandzeni (native title: Ngwnyama), an act that according to African understanding is merely seen as a right of use, but was understood by the whites as a transfer of ownership. In the year 1890, the land became a co-protectorate of the Cape Province and Transvaal. After the defeat of Transvaal in the Boer War (1899-1902), Swaziland became a British protectorate under the High Commissioner of South Africa and in 1968 achieved independence.

According to Swazi tradition, power does not lie solely with the King (Ingwnyama: "Lion") but also with the Queen Mother (Indovukazi: lit. "Great She-Elephant"). They are jointly responsible for the judicial system and the army. The situation has repeatedly caused tension, even to the extent of children being murdered.

The Royal Kraal, the parliament building, and the National Museum situated in a pretty garden where

the Swazi Stone-Age culture is also documented all lie in a valley to the south of the vacation resort Ezulweni, the Lobamba Royal Village. Ezulweni itself tries to attract guests with good hotels, golf courses and tennis courts as well as the casino. During apartheid, Swaziland was a refuge for mixed-race couples from South Africa and Zimbabwe (then Rhodesia), which provided a constant flow of hard currency for the country. But since the end of apartheid, the luxury hotels, sports facilities, gaming casinos and thermal spas are less and less frequented. And so the previously well-constructed roads are full of potholes, and the markets and accommodation have adapted to the general standard of South Africa.

The traveler who has little time will generally make only a brief visit to the capital city of Mbabane, on the River Mbabane (Bitter River). The city developed from the settlement that grew up at the trading post opened by Michael Wells in 1888 and today offers excellent shopping facilities. On Miller Street there are pretty shops and boutiques and modern government buildings, and at the southern end of the street is the Swazi market, which used to be of interest for its handcrafted products. However, today the impression is more one of a rundown market for cheap goods. For many years the goldmine at Pigg's Peak, 67 kilometers (42 miles) from the capital city and discovered in 1884 by William Pigg, was the largest in Swaziland. The small town dating from the gold rush era is now a center of the logging industry and has a picturesque market. The luxurious hotels are mostly neglected and no longer make a profit. Thirteen kilometers (8 miles) northeast, however, the spectacular Phophonyane Waterfalls cascade into the depths, a natural backdrop for a number of dramatic movies.

Manzini, the largest city and commercial center of the country, is also the home of the combined University of Swaziland, Lesotho and Botswana. Here, the tourist will find not only good hotels and tourist infrastructure, but also a variety of shopping facilities. At the foot of the Lebombo Mountains lie settlements of corrugated iron huts, wooden shacks and traditional round huts. Gentle hilly meadows, where cattle graze, and sugarcane plantations extend as far as the eye can see.

Cities, Pasture-lands, Waterfalls

Boer Country and Urban Centers in the North

From October to November, the avenues in Pretoria take on the violet hue of the blossoming trees (above). – The Heia Safari Ranch presents folklore shows and offers overnight accommodation (right). – From the viewpoint at World's End there is a dramatic view of the Blyde River Canyon (right-hand page).

In the midst of a splendid landscape and surrounded by the Magalies Mountains lies the city of Johannesburg. In the extravagant light of the African sun, the city's skyscrapers look like a pile of stones thrown together by chance in the middle of a trash heap. The city spreads its tentacles out into the surrounding highlands. Squashed in between skyscrapers and concrete blocks are the old historic facades. From the upper floors of some of the hotels you can see, not far from the center, the yellow, artificial gleam of hills – mine dumps of the 30 and more gold mines. The economic hub of the nation is literally built on gold; even below the city center there are kilometer-long mine tunnels. Gold Reef City, a gold mine museum in the style of the miners' settlements, gives the visitor the opportunity of viewing the underground passages of the gold mine, as well as seeing gold-smelting in progress and watching traditional tribal dances. Fanakalo, a new language, was created so that the different ethnic groups that constitute the mining workforce can communicate when working underground. It consists of many specialist mining terms and is understood by both whites and blacks. A few blocks north of the railway station in Johannesburg, the Chamber of Mines has erected a monument in honor of the gold miners, showing one white and two black miners at work.

Walking through Johannesburg by day, it feels as if you are in a large, often hectic metropolis where life never seems to stand still. In recent years, the inner city has become a "danger spot." Nowhere else in South Africa do the contrasts between rich and poor clash as dramatically as they do here. The wealthy whites have now moved out to the elegant suburbs, such as Sandton,

with its splendid villas, modern hotels and attractive shopping malls, or to Melville, three kilometers (two miles) northwest of the city center, with attractive cafés, restaurants and boutiques. Laughter, car horns and music can be heard there. Yuppies drift from bar to bar in the company of pretty girls. But the cheerful cosmopolitan atmosphere can easily lead you to forget that Johannesburg is surrounded by enormous townships. Compared with these "white" districts, the inner city, which has become almost uninhabitable because of the incidence of murder and theft, seems like a nightmare. The slum of Soweto (South Western Township), the largest settlement in South Africa that is exclusively inhabited by blacks, stretches for approximately 20 kilometers (13 miles) from the city center (10 kilometers/ 6 miles south of Johannesburg) over an area of 95 square kilometers (37 square miles). It has between approximately 2 and 3 million inhabitants and in some places more resembles a car graveyard or a trash dump than a residential settlement. The main feature of the district are the structures of corrugated iron and planks, piled together like boxes, barely offering protection from heat, rain or cold, but with one indispensable item: a television set.

But not all Soweto is a slum: in Masedi Street (Orlando West), the private villa of Nelson Mandela still stands, although it is a long time since he lived here. Unfriendly walls surround Winnie Mandela's 21-room villa. Just a stone's throw away, Archbishop Desmond Tutu used to live in a villa surrounded by high barbed wire – two Nobel Prize winners in one district. There are supposedly 12 millionaires in Soweto; some even say the number is 25. There is the huge Baragwanath Hospital; there are 362 schools, 300 churches and three cemeteries. Soweto also has a university, Vista University, where black students can take a degree. Three City Councils with exclusively black members are responsible for the administration of the 35 townships that make up Soweto. Approximately 4,000 police officers attempt to handle security issues. Anyway, as it is hopefully stated in the song "Sabela" by the larger-than-life singer Sibongile Khumalo from Soweto: "Now is the time to be happy. The sun is shining brightly. We are founding a nation. We are the power in the service of our land."

Gold Reef City is an amusement park with restaurants, a gold foundry and historic buildings (top). – Flea market fans will enjoy this Saturday market at the parking lot of the Market Theatre complex (above) where secular art and junk are on sale (right).

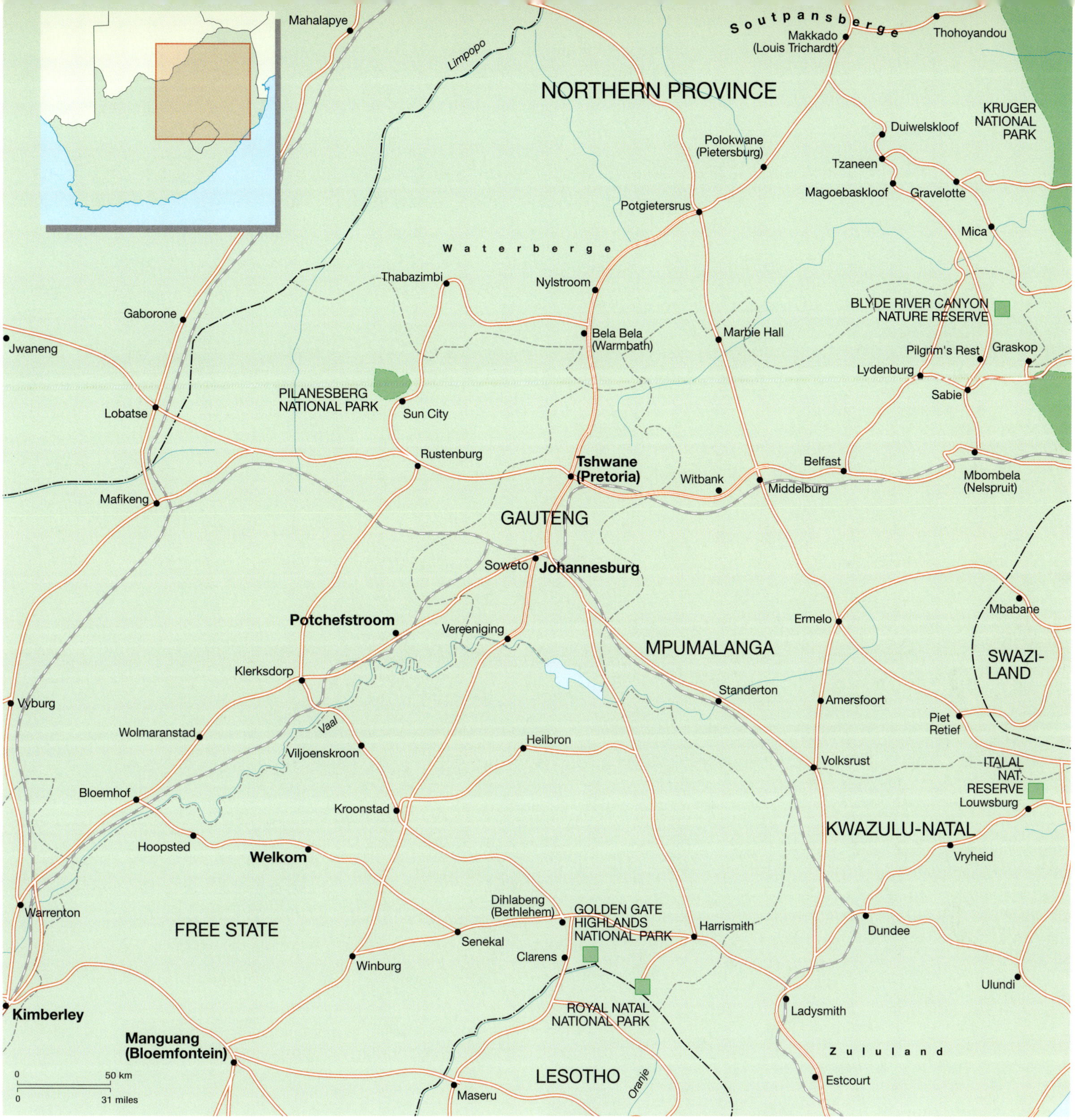

Tourists who fly from Johannesburg to the game parks or to the beaches by the Indian Ocean do not notice anything of this shocking contrast as they travel in their comfortable aircraft. How different it is when one travels overland, like Rian Malan, the author of the honest and critical book "My Traitor's Heart" (1990). He writes, "Approximately 16 kilometers beyond the last white city, one passes the border between the First and the Third World, between white South Africa and black KwaZulu. There is no border marking. It is not necessary. It is obvious that one is entering another country, another world." This is a different meaning of "the world in one country," namely one in which black and white correspond precisely to poor and rich.

The techniques of gold mining are demonstrated in a mine at Gold Reef City at a depth of approximately 220 meters (722 feet) (left).

Voortrekker Mentality in the Shade of Jacaranda Blossoms

Although they are only a half-hour's drive apart, whole worlds lie between Johannesburg and Pretoria, the capital city (alternating in this function every six months with Cape Town). Forming the administrative district of Tshwane along with the surrounding towns, the city of the early pioneers and Voortrekkers is a prosperous city, a "white" city, the city of government officials. Their houses, in the shade of ancient jacaranda trees, are hidden behind bougainvillea hedges, and in spring from October to November, the attractive buildings and avenues are enveloped in magnificent colors. Pretoria is not aggressive and noisy like Johannesburg; it is not a working class city, nor is it a booming metropolis, but a

The foundation stone of the Paul Kruger Dutch Reformed Church in Pretoria was laid in 1896 by the President of the Boers himself (large photo). – Union Buildings is the main seat of Parliament (left-hand page, bottom). Bronze figures at the plinth of the statue of Paul Kruger on Church Square symbolize the Boer defense force (below). – The Voortrekker Monument near Pretoria is like a block of brown granite (left).

neat and tidy colony of government officials where the mentality of the old Boers found fruitful soil right into the last years of the apartheid era. It is still scarcely possible for non-whites to acquire comfortable apartments or houses within the city, unless they are a member of the government, or very wealthy: since the end of apartheid, the increased property prices alone make sure of that. With its well-manicured lawns, innumerable pigeons and passing double-decker buses, Church Square seems very British. In the center stands a statue of the Boer leader, Paul Kruger (1825–1904). While the northern side of the Square is reminiscent of the Place de la Concorde in Paris, the south side is more like Trafalgar Square in London. The Meintjeskop above the city is dominated by the Union Buildings designed by Sir Herbert Baker (1862–1946). The long building of red sandstone, with red roof tiles, has two tall bell towers with small domes and monumental flights of steps. The two wings are intended to symbolize the languages English and Afrikaans. Besides the various government ministries, Union Buildings also houses various offices and the National Archives with valuable documents on the history of the country.

The Voortrekker Monument south of Pretoria is a massive structure of brown granite. It commemorates the bloody victory of the Boers over a Zulu force on December 16, 1838 and documents the history of the Great Trek, as well as the events that led to the battle at Blood River, in which only 464 Boers equipped with modern weapons massacred more than 3,000 Zulu. At the entrance to the tall granite building resting on a pediment there is a bronze statue of a mother protecting her two children. In the dome of the granite monument there is a hole through which, at midday on December 16, a ray of sun shines deep into the crypt, illuminating the cenotaph bearing the inscription: "Ons vir jou, Suid Afrika" ("We are for you, South Africa"). The entire monument is surrounded by a circle of stone wagons, a wall of 64 ox carts.

Venda – Land of the Rain Queen

A long time ago, the Boers with their heavily laden ox carts passed through a region full of natural beauty north of Pretoria. This is historic country, with old ruins and fanciful legends. Large areas are completely untouched, allowing the crystal-clear trout streams, huge waterfalls and dense primeval forest to be enjoyed in peace.

The Boers thought they had arrived in paradise and called this enchanting region Venda, which means something like "pretty country." Here they wanted to start a new life. But the region was inhabited by a people that today still practices the ancient rites of animism and reveres the python as holy. Towards the end of the 19th century, a pregnant woman was still drowned once a year in the mysterious Lake Funduzi, the spiritual shrine of the Venda, as a sacrifice to appease the Great Python. This is the realm of the Rain Queen who was portrayed in the novel "She" by Henry Rider Haggard (1856–1925).

The town of Vredenburg was founded as early as 1852, and in 1854 was renamed Potgietersrus in honor of General Piet Potgieter. This leader of the Voortrekkers was ambushed in the area

near Mooiddrift by members of the Ndebele tribe; several trekkers were killed. Approximately 1,500 Ndebele died afterwards, mainly from hunger and thirst, in the cave at Makapansgats, to which they had fled after the ambush. Beyond Louis Trichardt, at the foot of the Soutpansberg Mountains, lies an area of savanna with high grass and scattered cacti and groves of trees. The town was at first called Zoutpansbergdorp, but was then renamed for one of the famous Voortrekker leaders who moved on north from here in the 19th century. A memorial commemorates a meeting of the Boers whom he was leading with the Portuguese and with the tribe of the Shangaan. After violent conflicts with Venda warriors in 1898 the town was rebuilt in its present day form.

Tzaneen lies on the edge of the subtropical lowveld on the banks of the wide Letaba River. It is a colorful town and a center for the cultivation of citrus fruits, peanuts, tobacco and cotton. The name of the town comes from the Zonga word "in the basket" and aptly describes the situation of the town, as it lies in a valley.

The cliffs on the northern side of the imposing Drakensberg mountains are almost vertical (large photo). A pass road leads to the breathtaking Strijdom Tunnel where vendors offer their goods (above). – The high cliffs of the Abel Erasmus Pass make a striking scene (right).

On the Panorama Route

Traveling from the highveld to the lowveld, you will observe the way the sparse bush and shrub savanna gradually replaces the dense greenhouse vegetation around Tzaneen. Enormous baobabs appear along the roadside. Then a mountain rises up out of the dry plain, like a giant dome. The road climbs steadily past magnificent views to the 132-meter-long (433-foot) Strijdom Tunnel. The road across the pass climbs even higher, leading between the steep cliffs to the Abel Erasmus Pass. Gorges, valleys and green hillsides line the route as it climbs to a height of almost 1,200 meters (3,937 feet). The rugged sides of the massive cliffs of the Drakensberg Mpumalangas tower over canyons and gorges of breathtaking beauty. The Olifants and Blyde Rivers flow through the deep valleys of mudstones, dominated by the pinnacles, walls and castle-like rocks of the harder quartzite outcrops. A band of fast-growing pine and eucalyptus trees winds its way up into the mountains, sometimes resembling a Black Forest landscape. These forests have only been established in recent years; they draw large quantities of water from the ground and, as a large area of monoculture, are susceptible to bush fires and infestation by pests. In two places, the view is so overwhelming that one could almost feel that the entire universe is spread out at one's

See page 114

The Three Rondavels in late afternoon sunshine.

From Hunting Preserve to Protected Area

The Kruger National Park

The Kruger National Park is one of the highlights of a journey to southern Africa. The animal world there is overwhelming, whether waterbuck (2), African wild dogs, leopards (3) or resting cheetahs (5). From the Olifants Rest Camp in the central section of the Park there is a magnificent view across the savanna landscape (4). Lower Sabie Camp (1) in the south of the Park also offers overnight accommodation in pretty rondavels.

Giraffes sway strangely past, as if in slow motion. On the hilltops, gazelles keep a safe distance, ready to flee from a cheetah. A secretary bird, with its crest of long feathers at the back of its head, stalks with dignity across the savanna, but its apparent self-importance disappears with its clumsy takeoff when flying. When lightning flashes in the distance and a low rumbling signifies the approach of a thunderstorm, the endless plain suddenly fills up with the lowing of innumerable wildebeest. The ground trembles under the staccato rhythm of their hoofs. Amidst the lowing, one can hear the hoarse bark of the zebras. A buffalo herd races away in a wild gallop, and the earth shakes.

The Kruger National Park is one of the largest nature parks in the world, and possibly the most famous of them all. Nowhere else, not even in other parts of Africa, can a comparable number of animals be so comfortably observed in their wild state. As early as 1895, President Kruger (1825–1904) signed a document forbidding the hunting and killing of animals in the area that now forms the Kruger National Park. As you will often read in travel guides, this had less to do with the protection of the game than with being able to pursue his personal passion for hunting, even when the game in the surrounding regions had been totally decimated by the excessive hunt-

4

5

ing of white society. In 1902, the region which was previously known as the Sabie Nature Reserve was placed under the auspices of a Chief Gamekeeper, James Stevenson-Hamilton (1867–1957), a Scottish land owner and Major in the army who retained the post until he retired in 1946. He was totally lacking in experience when it came to the protection of endangered animal species, but he vigorously enforced the laws against poaching. He even brought a charge against a white police officer who had killed a wildebeest and who was then sentenced to a fine. In 1903, he was already in charge of three white and 50 black gamekeepers. He was soon given the nickname "Skukuza" ("He who sweeps clean"); now the name of one of the camps in the Kruger National Park.

In October 2001, within the context of the Peace Park Foundation projects, Nelson Mandela symbolically breached the fence between the Kruger National Park and the neighboring state of Mozambique, thus founding the Great Limpopo Transfrontier Park, which is still being developed. In future it will include the Kruger National Park in South Africa, the Gaza Park in Mozambique and the Gonarezhou National Park in Zimbabwe. In this way, the animals once again have free access to the whole territory, and at the same time safari tourism in all three countries will be enhanced.

To the west, the Kruger National Park adjoins a region in which various private game reserves are located (Timbavati, Klaserie, Tshukudu, Thornybush, Manyeleti, Sabi Sand, Londolozi, Mala Mala, Sabi Sabi and Inyati). These have exclusive lodges with a much more luxurious standard than those in the Kruger Park itself.

The tales of the adventures of the early European explorers still lure visitors today to go on safari. The once-hazardous undertaking has lost its element of danger. Tourists no longer have to do without comfort, and can move about almost without risk in a vast open-air zoo, very much in the tradition of the British colonial masters who created luxurious camps and transferred their own traditions to Africa.

Shades of color in the cliffs of the Blyde River Canyon Nature Reserve range from powder pink to russet (left). – Bourke's Luck Potholes at the confluence of the Blyde and Treur Rivers look like bizarre whirlpools (below and right-hand page).

feet. The fitting names of these two places are World's End and God's Window. The cult movie "The Gods Must Be Crazy" was filmed here. In the comfortable vacation resort of Blydepoort, one can watch the sunset, which happens very rapidly here. The rays of the sun glide along the slopes of the gorge; the undersides of the clouds are colored red for a while; and then the sky is illuminated briefly as if by a fire, although the sun has already set. A gentle breeze shakes the leaves of the trees and the secretive whispering of the African night begins.

The Panorama Route (or Summit Route) leads past basalt gorges that have been carved out over millions of years out by water erosion, passing three cones of rock that look like giant African huts. Some rock formations are even more impressive: Bourke's Luck Potholes, for example, which are cylinder-shaped holes in the rock which have now reached a depth of between two and three meters. Here, a treasure hunter named Bourke found gold, hence the name. In this area lies the confluence of the Blyde and Treur Rivers. Regarding the names of the rivers, the story is told that Andries Hendrik Potgieter (1792–1852) left his wagon trail in 1844 to try to find the Portuguese at Delegoa Bay. Weeks went past without any news of the Boer leader. Despondent, the Boers who had remained behind broke camp and named the river "Treurrivier," meaning "River of Mourning." But then Potgieter and his group caught up with them again, and they called the river where they were reunited "Blyderivier," "River of Joy."

Now a historic monument, the small gold-diggers' town of Pilgrims Rest authentically illustrates the life of the gold diggers. A gold digger known as Alec "Wheelbarrow" Patterson was the first person to find gold here, in 1873. The town with its 18 bars was

scarcely able to accommodate the large numbers of gold diggers of that time. When the deposits were nearly exhausted, the authorities purchased the abandoned facilities, and turned the ghost town into a haven of nostalgia.

The Panorama Route leads past a succession of beautiful waterfalls. At the Berlin Falls, for example, water flows through a natural lock before cascading some 80 meters (262 feet) into the dark green lagoon. Further to the west, the Lisbon Falls are also worth seeing. The water rushes over green cliffs into a glittering pool, 92 meters (302 feet) below. The name of the MacMac Falls can be traced to the many Scots who stayed in a camp here to look for diamonds and whose names all began with "Mac." You can climb steps to a projecting rock about halfway up, from where there is an excellent view of the waterfall. There are also beautiful waterfalls at Hazyview (Sabie Falls, Horse Shoe Falls, Forest Falls). The town is also the starting point for crossing the Long Tom Pass. Named after the "Long Tom" cannons that were used in the Boer War, it climbs to 2,149 meters (7,050 feet). A replica of one of the cannons can be seen at Devil's Staircase. There are plenty of viewing points from which you can enjoy the magnificent landscape characterized by the red of the soil and the green of the forests. The wide savannas of the Kruger National Park are not far away.

The little town of Sabie lies at the foot of Mount Anderson and the Mauchberg on the Sabie River. It is also known as the "Pearl of East Transvaal" because of its glorious location on the high plateau. Lydenburg's name ("Town of Suffering") refers to the tribulations endured by the trekkers before reaching the delightful valley in the heart of this mountainous world, and because of

Sun City – The "Las Vegas" of South Africa

Sun City, built in 1977 in the hollow of a volcanic crater near Rustenberg, used to be referred to as Sin City, because during apartheid many whites traveled from prudish South Africa to what was then the homeland Bophuthatswana in order to have a good time and to indulge in the gambling that was forbidden in the Boer state. The complex of buildings known as Lost City with the fairytale "Palace Hotel" is the fulfillment of millionaire Sol Kerzner's dream of building a golden castle. This enormous vacation resort has a gambling casino, a stadium for pop concerts, several sports grounds and two of the best golf courses in Africa, as well as numerous discos, bars, restaurants and pools, in a location beside lakes and rivers. There is a tropical rainforest with waterfalls and a wave pool, as well as the "volcanic" Bridge of Time that erupts once an hour. The illusion is complete when the sounds of the jungle come through the loudspeakers. This make-believe world is presented so convincingly that – as is often said in mockery – the visitors believe that even the full moon is not real.

The Berlin Falls (left-hand page, bottom) and the MacMac Falls (below) are just two examples of some of the waterfalls and their plant life that are found along the Panorama Route (bottom). – Pinnacle Rock is a freestanding granite column (left-hand page, top) – From the viewpoint God's Window there is a magnificent panorama view of the lowveld (left).

Long Tom Pass with its magnificent panorama view (below and right). Sandstone building in Kroonstad (right-hand page, bottom). – In front of the Dutch Reformed Mother Church there is a statue of the Voortrekker, Sarel Cilliers (right-hand page, far right). The statue commemorating President Reitz in Bloemfontein (right-hand page, center).

the malaria in the lowveld that claimed many victims. In 1849, the town became the capital of the independent Boer Republic.

Boer Traditions in Managuang

To the southwest of Johannesburg, there is an endless expanse of meadows and arable land – the farming land of the Boers. This pleasant region is the historical, and also the conservative heartland of the country. The towns here have German, Dutch or biblical names (such as Bethlehem), and vast fields of sunflowers alternate with wheat, flax and corn. Most of the buildings have Cape Dutch features and are built of sandstone; farmhouses appear defiant, almost fortress-like. On the southern bank of the Vaal River is the popular vacation resort of Parys, with a range of leisure facilities, golf courses, tennis courts and camp sites. After passing through yet another corn-growing area, you will reach the town of Kroonstadt, founded in 1855. During the Boer War (1899–1902) it was temporarily the capital of the Boer Republic of that time, the Orange Free State.

Bloemfontein, the "judicial capital" and third capital city of South Africa, was founded in 1840. it has recently changed its name to Manguang ("City of the Cheetahs"). The capital city of the Free State and the principal traffic hub was once an estate with the name Bloem Fonteyn ("Fountain of Flowers"). It has a number of

interesting buildings, including The Old Presidency in the Scottish Baronial style; the massive Victorian Supreme Court; and the red-brick building of the Fourth Raadsaal with white domes and columns in the style of a Greek temple, where the last Boer government assembled before the British occupation. The Court of Appeal is also an attractive building with Italian roof tiles and windowsills and a portico supported by four columns and approached by a flight of stairs. Inside, the courtroom has magnificent black stinkwood paneling. The domed building of the City Hall has a notable columned portico; the central tower has a pretty carillon. The history of the city was characterized by battles, in particular those between the Boers and the armies of the British Cape region. The methods of the latter were none too gentle; they imprisoned the Boer women and children, about 26,000 in number, in internment camps and let them die of thirst in the scorching sun. The National Women's Memorial and War Museum of the Boer Republics commemorates the Boer War and the concentration camps of that period. In the grounds there is a 36-meter-high (118-foot) obelisk with bronze figures showing a mother with her dying child in her arms and a young woman who is looking with hope into the future. At the foot of the obelisk, the ashes of Emily Hobhouse are buried. She was an English lady who cared for the prisoners and confronted the British government with their suffering. The confrontations between the Boers and the Sotho people here were also cruel. The privileges that were fought for then are defended all the more relentlessly today. Although the white population has taken notice of the abolition of apartheid, it seems that it has scarcely followed it through with action.

Manguang (Bloemfontein) is the capital city of the Free State.

A Last Paradise

Endangered Botswana

The Okavango Delta, a maze of swamps and lakes, is a tourist highlight in Botswana (1). – 2 Letchwe antelope find sufficient food in the delta. 3 A Herero settlement near Maun. 4 A rustic camp in the Moremi Game Reserve. – 6 The sausage tree (kigelia) gets its name from its elongated fruit.

There is good road access into Botswana, as well as regular flights. Seen from the air, the landscape looks like a worn carpet with a yellow-red weave and irregular creases. Small black trees, either burnt or withered, are scattered at wide intervals. Now and again you will see a dead-straight road that disappears over the horizon. Unlike the journeys of the early 19th-century missionaries and explorers like David Livingstone (1813–1873), who walked throughout what was then known as Bechuanaland equipped only with the Bible and a gun, a visit to the Delta today requires considerable organizational effort. Large four-wheel-drive vehicles that transport baggage and provisions for a whole week cross the Thamalakane River near Maun and continue along the sandy tracks as far as possible towards the waters of the Okavango. On both sides of the track, termite hills rise meter-high from the ground. The adjoining Moremi Game Reserve was founded in 1963 and now encompasses almost 5,000 square kilometers (1,930 square miles). It includes almost one-third of the Okavango Delta. Chobe National Park in the far north also offers excellent opportunities for animal-watching. The Okavango River meanders through a network of swamps, lakes and lagoons and alters its course from year to year. Before it seeps away in the desert, it creates a true paradise. From the onset of the rains in Angola between January and March, it takes another two months until the Okavango rises to become a mighty river 300

meters (984 feet) wide and three meters (10 feet) deep, and until the increased volume of water that it is carrying reaches the southern part of the Delta. The period with the most water more or less coincides with the season of greatest aridity in the Sahel climate of Botswana. The dryness of the desert thus meets with tropical humidity. When the water from the Okavango spreads out through the Kalahari and floods an entire region, the vegetation grows with a luxuriance that is not seen anywhere else in the drought-plagued regions of Africa. This huge wetland biotope is like a Land of Cockaigne for the African fauna that congregate here. But even paradise is endangered. Plans by the neighboring state of Namibia could have disastrous results. Only a few kilometers from the border with Botswana, the electric power company of Namibia, NamPower, is planning to construct a huge dam in the Caprivi Strip, near the Popa waterfalls, to use the water from the Okavango to produce electric power. This would have unimaginable consequences for Botswana, as the sediments that are normally washed into the Delta would then be lacking. However, these minerals are essential for the unique species there. In addition, the huge volumes of water that until now are transported into the Delta and the Kalahari would be drastically reduced. The dammed-up Okavango would be transformed into a lethargic, evenly flowing river that would no longer have the power to flood large regions. Huge areas would be turned into steppe, and the habitat of the animal world would shrink dramatically. It would signal the end of an entire river system and thus of the last original animal protection zone in the world. The electric power produced would be sufficient for only 25,000 households in Namibia, but would cost approximately 33 million euros and deprive 100,000 people in Botswana of the basis of their existence.

Sandstone Arches and Wild Flowers

South Africa's "Wild West"

Red dunes under deep blue sky are typical for the landscape near Bokspits (above). Quiver trees can also be seen along the Oranje River near Upington (right). Upstream from the Augrabies Falls the Oranje River crashes into an enormous rock basin (right-hand page).

Traveling north from Cape Town towards Namibia, the landscape does not offer very much variety. The icy-cold water of the Benguela Current does not evaporate, causing the clouds to roll in from the ocean towards the coast and producing the typical sea mist. This forms every evening on the surface of the cold ocean, only to be dispersed by the warm rays of the sun the following morning. The "Wild West" of South Africa, the Northern Cape and the northern area of the Western Cape, has the reputation of being of interest only to fans of untamed and rugged landscapes, storm-beaten cliffs and deserts. There are no cities; the wilderness reigns supreme. For long distances the unspoiled landscape consists of salt plains and semi-deserts. Here there are only a few roads and tracks that stretch endlessly in a straight line to the horizon. But another aspect of the "Wild West" – as in North America – is the gold and diamond rush. In 1866, here in South Africa, a young man with the biblical name of Stephanus Erasmus Jakob picked up a stone in the vicinity of a small place called Hopetown and found it glinted more than the others. It was a magnificent 21-carat diamond. Not long afterwards, a shepherd found another diamond nearby weighing 85.5 carats. These two finds were the starting signal for the craziest diamond rush of the 19th century. People dug deep down into the ground and heaped up piles of soil containing all kinds of minerals. The prosperous settlement of Kimberley with its large mine was founded during this period of diamond fever. But only small numbers of travelers visit this town on the "Diamond Route."

Wildflowers in Namaqualand

Bizarre succulents have learnt to live with drought. Once a year, however, the semi-desert blossoms. After the first rains, when Namaqualand is covered with a vast carpet of colorful flowers that envelopes these otherwise dry hills from August until October, then the region resembles huge ocean of flowers. All the tour operators have this "Miracle of the Desert" in their program. The few guesthouses along the coast are booked out, and the camp sites overcrowded. Even though the enthusiasm of the many visitors is usually directed towards the "flower miracle," there are many other interesting things to see in this region. For example, wine. The vines have to withstand the constant bitter wind, and the grapes ripen very slowly. The sunshine, though not excessive, is very intense because it is reflected from the cliffs and gives the wine from Vredendal its typical concentrated flavor. And then there is the food: in numerous skerms (outdoor restaurants) along the coast you can try seafood – black mussels the size of the palm of your hand, oysters, lobster, fish, grilled, baked or made into delicious soup. In the wild, bare and rugged West, at least you do not have to go hungry.

At first, granite blocks and sparse shrub vegetation are scattered throughout the landscape, but the further north one travels, the rockier and more barren it becomes. In the northern, sun-drenched valley, the shadows creep over wavy hills that appear on the glimmering horizon like dark islands. The fertile fruit growing region of Ceres is located along the Dwars River, surrounded by mountains. It has the largest fruit-packing plant in the southern hemisphere. The main cultivation area for apples is also a popular vacation spot because of its picturesque location, and in winter the Matroosberg Range even offers facilities for winter sports. Tulbagh, founded in 1699, still has many beautiful houses dating from the 18th century, especially gabled houses with luxuriant, subtropical front gardens. The Oude Kerk (1743) is thought to be the oldest Protestant church of the southern hemisphere; today it is used as a museum.

The Cedarberg Mountains, stretching for 100 kilometers (63 miles) between Citrusdal and Clanwilliam and reaching heights of up to 2,028 meters (6,654 feet), have been placed under protection as the Cedarberg Wilderness Area. A typical feature of the vegetation of the Cedarbergs is fynbos, an extremely thrifty and resistant hard-leaved evergreen shrub. This is the only place where the unique snow protea grows above the snow line. The rugged peaks of the Cedarbergs ride high above a land covered

North of Cape Town there is a delightful landscape full of proteas, heather and wild flowers (top). The Big Hole in Kimberley is a crater dug out by human hand for the extraction of diamonds (above). – Birds find plenty of space to live and breed in the vicinity of plantations, gardens and small reservoirs near Upington (right).

Near Upington (bottom). Water wheels are still in use near Keimoes and Kakamas. Church at Keimoes (top).

with bushes and dissected by rivers, where wind and weather have carved out a landscape of sandstone arches and bizarre sculptures. A permit is required to enter the nature reserve, but there is scarcely a region in Western South Africa that is more fascinating than this, with its cedar forests, rivers, valleys and strange mountain landscapes. The Wolfberg Arch is a spectacular example of the power of erosion. Lying in untouched valleys with crystal-clear streams, the steep-walled rock formations

Large herds of wildebeest range through the barren Kalahari searching for food (large photo). Springboks enjoy the greenery on the sparse bushes (left-hand page, bottom). – The oryx antelope is known in South Africa as the gemsbok (left)

Robert Moffat – and Mary Livingstone

Born on December 21, 1795, the Scottish missionary, Robert Moffat, was responsible for the best-known mission station of the London Missionary Association in Southern Africa. Established in Kuruman from 1826, it was named the "Source of Christianity." Moffat built the simple church, at that time the largest building in the interior, and translated the Bible into the Setswana language, which previously had no written form, for his Tswana mission pupils. In 1831, he printed the New Testament in this language, using a hand printing press. He explored Matabele Land (present-day Zimbabwe) and was an experienced gardener. His daughter Mary, who was born in Griquatown in 1820, married the famous Africa pioneer explorer, David Livingstone (1813–1873) in 1845. She died in 1862 and Robert Moffat died on August 9, 1883. The dwelling house, a school building and the church now serve as a museum. The mission is considered the starting point for Livingstone's journeys of exploration "into the darkest Africa."

with their strangely chiseled forms provide a paradise for hikers and photographers.

Tea, Sheep and Rock Drawings

This region is referred to as the "largest open air art gallery in the world"; with 130 locations with rock paintings, this is certainly no exaggeration. Artistic stone drawings of the Khoikhoi and the San can be seen on rock overhangs and in caves. Some of the pictures in the Swartberg Mountains are said to be 6,000 years old. In 1989, a small group of San returned here in order to live in an artificially created settlement. This is a private game enclosure called Kagga Kamma, and the village has an adjoining lodge. Some of the original inhabitants had roles in Jamie Muy's movie "The Gods Must Be Crazy." The first white settlers in South Africa, the Dutch, gave the name "bosjemans" to the diminutive,

yellow-skinned and narrow-eyed people, who are less than 1.60 meters (5 feet 3 inches) tall. The name, which means something like loafer or lazy-bones, was presumably the origin of the name Bushman. Ethnologists refer to them as the San. A particular feature of this people is that their skin is extremely wrinkled, even that of the younger people. Their hair grows in little tight bundles. The Khoikhoi (Hottentots) and San (Bushmen) speak languages that are closely related to each other and are characterized by so-called click consonants.

On the east bank of the dammed-up Olifants River stands the town of Clanwilliam. It was founded in 1820 by Irish immigrants and named after the Earl of Clanwilliam (1795–1879). It is an atmospheric little place with pretty thatched houses dating from the period of its founding, a pleasant Main Street and attractive church.

Rafting, swimming and canoeing are the preferred sports at the Oudrif Guest Farm in a fertile valley not far away. The popular rooibos (red bush) tea is cultivated in this area. Rooibos tea is also produced further to the east in Wuppertal, founded in 1830 by Rhenish missionaries at the foot of the Cedarbergs. It is characterized by its high vitamin C content and its aromatic flavor. The best place for wine-tasting is in the Golden Valley Cellars near Vredendal.

The extensive wildflower reserve at Ramskop is famous for its orange-colored daisies, which bloom, depending on the rainfall, between July and September. Vanrhynsdorp is a sheep-breeding center and is famous for its large variety of cacti. Lying at the foot of the Matsikamma Table Mountain which rises 1,016 meters (3,333 feet) above the rooftops, the town is the gateway to southern Namaqualand. Calvinia, a little further to the east, is the capital of

A lonely trail winds through a white glistening salt pan (left). – Ostriches can also survive in the Kalahari (below). – One of the highlights of an African safari is an encounter with a leopard, one of the most splendid representatives of the "Big Five;" this photo shows a leopard under an acacia tree in the Kalahari (right)

the northwestern Cape and also the center of the Hantam region and of the wool-producing industry of South Africa. The Art-Deco style synagogue serves as a reminder that the population once included a significant proportion of Jews. Hantam House can be visited by prior arrangement, as can the private house at Bothasdal with its collection of 17th and 18th-century furniture. The South African War Memorial to the west of Calvinia commemorates the last battle between the Boers and the British.

Continuing further north towards Upington, you will pass through the Sak River valley, where there is a monument commemorating the Great Trek of 1838 at Brandvlei. Extensive areas of salt pans characterise the flat high plateau. Dorper sheep, a breed famous in particular for its meat and wool, gather beside the watering holes of the sheep farms, which are marked by wind pumps. Even further north lies the area known as Kokerboom Forest. Here are the largest stands of the quiver tree in the Cape Province. They owe their name to the San who used the branches to carve quivers for their arrows. Arriving at Kenhardt after a seemingly endless journey, you will discover a center where Karakul sheep are bred and mutton is produced. The land here is as flat as a billiard table; the road cuts a straight line through the landscape. The journey continues to Keimoes in the lower valley of the Oranje River. Here a large water wheel is still operating and is preserved as an historic monument. Kakamas, surrounded by wheatfields and date palms, looks like an oasis with its old water wheels still working. The road then crosses the Oranje River and

See page 136

Rock drawings testify to a culture which is more than 1,000 years old.

The "Big Five"

Rulers of the Animal World

Travelers consider themselves lucky if they manage to see a member of the "Big Five."
1 White rhinoceros (Hluhluwe Reserve)
2 A pride of lions in the Kalahari.
3 A herd of elephants in Addo Elephant Park.
4 Buffalo (Hluhluwe Reserve)
5 Leopard (Kruger National Park).

When Africa was still a hunting paradise for white trophy collectors, the tusks of elephants, the horns of rhinoceroses and buffalos, and the skins of lions and leopards were highly prized. Well able to defend themselves, these animals were called The Big Five. Since hunting is now largely forbidden, travelers and keen photographers consider themselves happy simply to encounter these five varieties of animal during a safari.

The "King of the Animals" is the lion, the largest big cat of Africa and the only variety of big cat that lives and hunts in prides. Males remain with the pride only until they are about 18 months old and are then driven off by stronger rivals. When the latter take over a pride, they may kill the offspring of their predecessor. Sometimes three or four young males join together and live as bachelors in a hunting pack. Lions are not particularly good at long pursuits. Whereas female lions are provided for by other females if they are seriously hurt, injury for a male means that it will be hunted and finally torn apart and killed by hyenas.

The African elephant's most important organ is its trunk. It is both a sensitive organ of touch, with a fine sense of smell, and also an instrument for grasping and sucking. The tusks are used for fighting or to remove the bark of trees and for digging up roots. The large, triangular-shaped ears are

used as a fan for cooling the body. Vigorous waving of the ears can also be a threatening gesture. The lifespan of the animals depends on the condition of their lower jaw. When the last of their three generations of teeth are worn away, elephants die of hunger. Bulls must leave the herd at the age of between 10 and 12 years, and then form small herds with other young males; or they sometimes roam through the land as moody loners. When fleeing, they form a group, gathering the young animals protectively into the center.

The horn of the rhino does not consist of bone, but (like hooves and nails) of a dense structure of keratin fibers. The black rhino has a prehensile finger-shaped extension of its upper lip that it uses to pluck leaves. It does not see well, but has an excellent sense of hearing and smell. An attacking rhino stretches out its tail, and an animal that is about to flee holds its tail erect and bent slightly forwards; it runs with its head held high. The calf of a black rhino will generally follow its mother. White rhinos eat only grass and herbs. They have a blunt, square upper lip without the prehensile "finger." They are heavier than black rhino and the head is longer and larger. They are not as likely to attack as black rhino. Leopards are identified by their grey-yellow or ocher-colored skin with black rosette-shaped rings. They sleep in trees during the day and hunt mainly at night. They are loners and drag their victims into the trees to guard them from their rivals. Leopards do not like hunting. If they do not catch their prey immediately, they let it escape.

Buffalos are the epitome of concentrated strength. They live in herds of up to 1,000 cows, calves and young bulls. Older bulls are often loners and seek out fertile hunting areas near water, where they can graze at night and rest under a tree during the hot part of the day, or take a mud bath. Buffalos have wide horns that turn outwards and that grow together in the middle, forming a bulge on the forehead.

135

The huts of the Himba consist of a structure of sticks, covered with a mixture of clay and cattle dung (right-hand page, bottom). – Himba woman with children at Kaókoveld in northern Namibia, on the border with Angola (far right). – The most noticeable adornment of the Himba women is a white, cone-shaped shell that is worn between the bare breasts (right).

follows the south bank for 10 kilometers (6 miles) before leaving the river and turning southwest. After another turn to the right, it rejoins the river again. Near Alheit, a right-hand turn leads to the town of Augrabies and then on to Augrabies Falls National Park.

The Place of Great Noise – Augrabies Falls

During the course of approximately one billion years, the Oranje River has worn away its bed and cut deep into the ancient granite and gneiss rocks near Augrabies Falls, aptly called Aukoerebis (Place of Great Noise) by the Khoikhoi. Above the waterfalls, the main branches of the river merge and then drop from the 56-meter-wide (184 feet) granite plateau into the 147-meter-deep (482 feet) and 15-kilometer-long (9 miles) gorge. Here the river flows over more steep gradients, forming a series of spectacular rapids. The waterfalls in Augrabies Falls National Park are among the six largest waterfalls in the world and are particularly spectacular during the southern summer between October and March. As you watch the seething water below in the gorge from a rocky projection, the mud-colored water throws up a haze of white spray and creates a magnificent rainbow. If you plan a long hike in the vicinity of this natural spectacle you should exercise care. Although the air feels cool thanks to the fine spray, the sun still shines mercilessly, so it is essential to take plenty of water and to wear a head covering. Nonetheless, a hike here should not be missed: the ground glistens and glimmers almost everywhere with semi-precious stones such as rose quartz, tiger's eyes and tourmalines.

Sultanas, Port and Sherry

Surprises await you as you follow the Oranje River northwards. Just now, the landscape consisted of nothing but desert; suddenly the banks of the longest river in South Africa are covered in lush

greenery. Vines alternate with apricot plantations, pineapple groves and peach gardens, with date palms and mango trees. The air is heavy with the scent of ripe fruit. Surrounded by this extravagance of nature, the outline of a small town comes into view. This is Upington, the "Afrikaner City," an agricultural center producing almost 80 percent of all raisins and currants sold in Europe, as well as 84 percent of all South African table grapes. 750 wine growers have joined together to form the Oranje River Cooperative Wine Cellars; they supply more than half of the world's dessert wines. Sherry and port also produced here. Thanks to a system of canals, the town is surprisingly green, although it lies at the edge of the desert. It was founded by the Rev. Christiaan Wilhelm Heinrich Schroeder in 1875 as a Dutch Reformed mission station known as Olyvenhoudtsdrift. Some years later, the settlement was re-named after Sir Thomas Upington (1844-1898), who at that time was Attorney General of the Cape Colony. The former church building is now part of the Kalahari-Oranje Museum in Schroeder Street.

The Land of Red Dunes – The Kalahari

Upington is the starting point for an adventurous journey through the barren desert landscape in the direction of Botswana. The bizarre shape of a strange tree will fascinate you as you head northwards. Halfmensboom (Half Person Tree) is the name of a variety of tree aloe that can grow to a height of nine meters (30 feet). With the main stem in the center and the "arms" stretched upwards at an angle, it is easy to understand the derivation of the name. In the Kalahari, some of the San still live as nomads. These small figures, clothed only with a loincloth, can sometimes be seen along the roads.

The sand dunes near Bokspits seem to have become frozen into little billowing waves. These red-colored wandering dunes are as high as mountains with valleys, and reach far beyond the horizon. In the glimmering heat, numerous mirages hasten over the plains. The dunes rumble when the wind blows the sand away too quickly, and the ocean of sand begins to heave; then it seems as if a storm is approaching and the air is veiled with fine particles of dust. Built on telegraph poles, huge nests of the weaver bird border the roadside like works of art. Following the course of the border with Botswana, a barbed wire fence, the route leads towards Andriesvale and then to the entrance of the vast park which was formed in 1999 by amalgamating the South African Kalahari Gemsbok National Park and the Gemsbok National Park in Botswana. Now called the Kgalagadi Transfrontier Park, since its opening the animals are free to follow their old migratory paths, since the border between South Africa and Botswana is in most places now only indicated by white stones. This extensive game reserve provides an impression of the fascinating landscape of the Kalahari, with its chain of orange-red dunes, the white-yellow savanna plains and the unique animal world that has adapted to the dry savanna environment. The camp for safari tourists is called Twee Rivieren, meaning "Two Rivers." One of these, the Nossob River, which is normally marked as long and wide on the maps, turns out in reality to be a dry river bed for most of its length, only recognizable because the vegetation here is a little denser. The second river, the Auob, transforms its banks into blossoming slopes only every two or three years; most of the time it remains an empty promise. Everywhere there are thorn bushes that seem to crackle in the dryness. Between the "rivers," in a region known as the Inner Veld, lie the sand dunes of the Kalahari, as red as the Venetian red on the palette of a painter. Occasionally

Weaver bird nest in the Kalahari (top). – Bottle tree (above). – In the semi-desert of Namibia, you need to be a good walker (right-hand page, top). – Aloe bush (right-hand page, bottom)

one sees acacias, shepherd's trees and the grey camel thorn. Blackthorn, raisin bush, driedoring (three-thorn) and desert plants, such as the tsamma (wild) melon and wild cucumber – a delicacy for the gemsboks – grow near the river beds. There are the huge nests of the sociable weaver birds, one of the 215 varieties of birds in the park, in the camel thorn trees – a misnomer: since "kameelperd" means giraffe in Afrikaans, they should really be called "giraffe thorn." North of Twee Rivieren, the heat of the day becomes overpowering. Grass and bushes are sparse. The sand dunes extend to the horizon like the waves of a dried out ocean. It is as hot as an oven. Bush and umbrella acacias grow on ocher-colored sand dunes; dry watercourses peter out somewhere in the shimmering heat. The Kalahari is especially magnificent after the rare rainfall, when under a deep blue sky the rich green of the acacias contrasts brilliantly with the red dunes and the water-filled white clay pans.

Sossusvlei: the land of gentle dunes.

German Footprints in the Sand

A Detour to Namibia

1 Team of oxen in Damaraland. 2 Numerous seals gather at Cape Cross – 3 In the middle of the highest Namib dunes lies the Sossusvlei depression, which has no natural outlet. – 4 A dead tree in the Kalahari is used by a weaver bird as a nesting place – 5 The rock engravings at Twyfelfontein (Namibia) are up to 6,000 years old.

From South Africa, it makes sense to consider making a side trip to Namibia. There are good roads leading north and regular flights into Windhoek, which still unmistakably demonstrates its German colonial character. Kaiser-Wilhelm-Strasse may have been renamed Independence Avenue after independence in 1990, but the Equestrian Memorial on Robert Mugabe Avenue (previously Leutweinstrasse) still commemorates only the German soldiers who fell during the "Herero and Hottentot Rebellion 1903 to 1907." During that time, tens of thousands of Herero died of hunger and thirst, and thousands of prisoners died of disease in camps run by the German "Protection Force." Only at a commemorative ceremony on August 14, 2004, did the German Minister for Economic Cooperation and Development, Heidemarie Wieczorek-Zeul, apologize for these atrocities. And yet, married Herero women still wear the long skirts and head covering in the style of the missionary wives of the 19th century. An even greater paradox for Black Africa is the German atmosphere in Swakopmund,

which has a Poststrasse (Post Office Road) lined with palm trees, a neo-Baroque Lutheran church, a railway station in the colonial style and a red-and-white lighthouse. In "Cafe Anton," you can eat German apple pie or Black Forest gateau. The waiter (still black, of course) will take your order in fluent German.

The region north of Swakopmund, where the Atlantic crashes on the rocky coastline, is known as the Skeleton Coast because of the wrecks of numerous ships that were stranded or capsized off the coast. Fine sand beaches stretch for many kilometers and are strewn with weathered wooden beams, packing cases, metal drums and other flotsam and jetsam.

The region between the Swakop River in the north and the Kuiseb River in the South is known as the Namib. Here gravel plains typify the landscape, interrupted only occasionally by an isolated mountain. Approximately in the center, south of the Kuiseb, is the most spectacular desert landscape of the Namib – the valley of dunes of Sossusvlei, a clay basin surrounded by enormous waves of sand. Behind these are wandering dunes that reach a height of 400 meters (1,312 feet) and are colored terracotta-red or honey-yellow. Nearby is the spectacular Dead Vlei with its white mud floor and dried-up camel thorn trees. Namibia also has retained a paradise for animals: Etosha National Park. This region of grass savanna that gives way to dry bush and thornbush savanna was declared a game protection area in 1907 by the German Governor, Friedrich von Lindequist. In the language of the Herero, Etosha means "the land of dry water" or "great white place." The heart of this landscape is the dry, silver-white gleaming plain of saliferous clay. At about 40 waterholes, there are good opportunities for watching wild animals.

Those who undertake a tour in a four-wheel-drive vehicle into Kaókoland in the north of the country will be rewarded by at least two highlights: an encounter with the Himba, the people of the "Red Shepherds," and the impressive Epupa waterfalls. The Himba women rub their body with butter mixed with a red powder made from rocks that contain iron and aromatic herbs. This provides protection from the intense sun and from insects. On the border with Angola, the thundering waters of the Kunene River crash over the falls and disappear into a gorge, to appear again as a mass of foaming spray and then continue their journey as a fast-flowing river.

143

Planning your Journey

Size/ Situation/ Region

With a total area of 1.2 million square kilometers (463,200 square miles), South Africa is approximately five times the size of the United Kingdom and almost twice the size of the U.S. state of Texas. In the north, South Africa has borders with Namibia, Botswana and Zimbabwe and in the northeast with Mozambique. Lesotho and Swaziland are enclaves surrounded by South African territory.

Population

The total population is 42.8 million. The vast majority is formed by the blacks with 77 percent. Colored and mixed-race people –

Dancer at the Heia Safari Ranch.

The beaches of Noordhoek are only suitable for riding or windsurfing.

most of whom live in Cape Province – form a much smaller group, making up only approximately 9 percent of the total. Whites comprise about 10 percent of the population. The Afrikaners, Afrikaans-speaking white South Africans (also known as Boers) make up 57 percent of the white population, with English-speaking South Africans making up about 37 percent.

Language

The cultural diversity of South Africa is reflected in the numerous languages and dialects. In the past, English and Afrikaans were the official languages. Today there are 11 official languages. For tourists, English is perfectly adequate in almost all regions.

Climate/ Best Time to Travel

The southern winter (northern hemisphere's summer) is the best time for traveling to most regions of South Africa, including the lowveld with the Kruger National Park and KwaZulu-Natal. As this is also the dry period, the animals congregate at waterholes, so conditions for observing them are good. In subtropical KwaZulu-Natal, the swimming season is from June to August. The best months for the Garden Route are April to May. The Tsitsikamma National Park can best be visited in June and July; here it rains frequently, particularly in March, August, October and November. In the highveld in the interior (above elevations of 2,000 meters/ 6,562 feet) and in the Drakensberg mountains, the temperatures in the southern winter often fall below freezing point at night, but the days are predominantly sunny. In Lesotho, nights in the southern winter can be frosty, but it almost never rains; June to November is a good time here. In Swaziland, the best time for traveling is between April and September; from October to March it rains throughout the entire land. From April to October is also a good time to visit Upington and the Augrabies Falls; the Kgalagadi Transfrontier Park enjoys sunny days with cold nights from March until October; from November to February, it is very hot and from January to April there is rainfall. The Western Cape has rains during the southern winter, not during the southern summer. In Cape Town, most rain falls between June and August, so that a visit here during the southern summer (October to March) is ideal.

Time Zones

South African time is 12 hours ahead of North American Pacific Time, 7 hours ahead of New York and 2 hours ahead of London (GMT). As South Africa stretches from the 17th to the 33rd degree of longitude, the sun rises or sets earlier in Durban than, for example, in Cape Town.

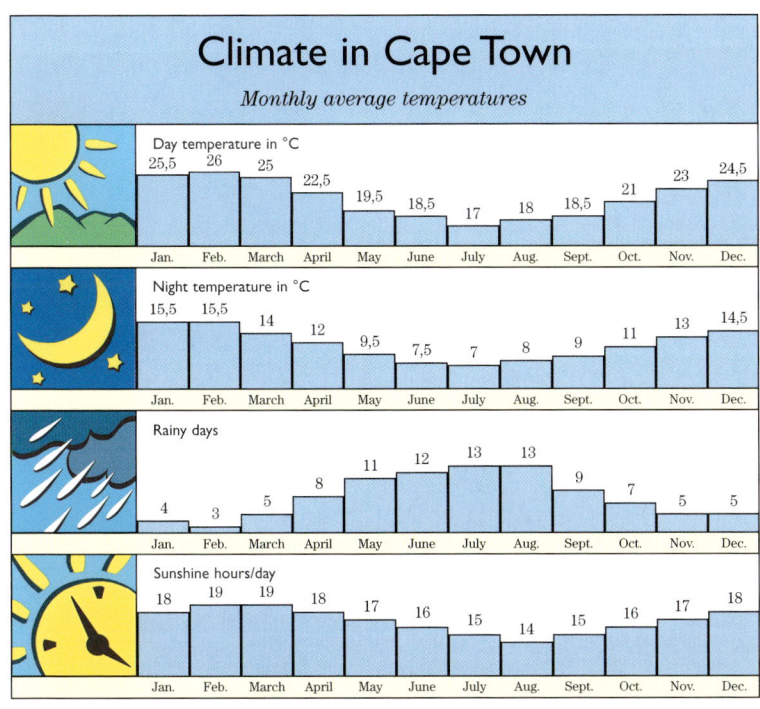

Public Holidays and Religious Festivals

March 21 (Day of Human Rights; commemorates the bloodbath in Sharpeville in 1960)
March/April (Good Friday, Easter Sunday, Easter Monday: Family Day)
April 27 (Freedom Day: commemorates the first free elections in 1994)
May (Ascension Day)
May 1 (Worker's Day/ Labor Day)
June 16 (Youth Day: commemorates the student uprising in Soweto in 1976)
August 9 (National Women's Day)
September 24 (Heritage Day; originally Shaka Day of the Zulu)
December 16 (Day of Reconciliation; originally Day of the Vow)
December 25 (Christmas Day)
December 26 (Day of Good Will)

A Zulu wearing leopard skins, a sign that he is a Chief.

Getting There

Johannesburg International Airport (JNB) is the major airport in South Africa and is the hub for 45 airlines from all five continents. Flights from Europe are generally overnight – an aperitif, dinner, sound sleep, and a good breakfast – and voilà, you're in South Africa! Direct flights between the U.S.A. and Johannesburg or Cape Town take about 15 hours, and flights between London and Johannesburg take about 12 hours. Further international airports are in Cape Town (CPT), Bloemfontein (BFN), Durban (DUR) and Port Elizabeth (PLZ).

The University of Cape Town lies at the foot of Table Mountain.

Medical Care

Medical care meets Western standards. Doctors' practices and pharmacies run out-of-hours emergency services in all the larger cities. As medical care must be paid for in cash, it is advisable to take out overseas medical insurance before traveling.

Information

The official South Africa Tourism Website is geared to international queries and has information available with specific relevance for almost every other country: www.southafrica.net
Telephone information/assistance in planning a trip:
UK: 0870 1550 044
Ireland: 01-6030996
Australia: 01-800-238643
USA: 1-800-593-1318
HEAD OFFICE:
Bojanala House,
90 Protea Road, Chislehurston,
Johannesburg 2196
Phone: + 27 (0)11 895 3000
Fax: +27 (0)11 895 3001
E-mail: info@southafrica.net
UNITED KINGDOM
Lebo Mokhesi, Manager: UK South African Tourism
6 Alt Grove London
SW19 4DZ
United Kingdom
PO Box 49110,

Wimbledon,
SW19 4XZ
United Kingdom
Phone: +44 (0) 20 8971 9350
Fax: +44 (0) 20 8944 6705
E-mail: info.uk@southafrica.net
UNITED STATES OF AMERICA
Dr Felicia Mabuza-Suttle
President
South African Tourism
500 5th Avenue
20th Floor,
Suite 2040,
New York NY 10110
Phone: +1 212 730 2929
Fax: +1 212 764 1980
E-mail: info.us@southafrica.net
LA office:
Phone: +1 310 643 6481
Fax: +1 310 643 0333

Swimming

On the east coast of South Africa, the warm Agulhas Current from the Indian Ocean makes for pleasant water temperatures. Apart from the rocky coast of the Tsitsikamma National Park, there are magnificent beaches. Between East London and Port Edward there may be sharks. The beaches to the north of Zinkwazi Beach are not secured with shark nets. It is not advisable to swim in inland lakes or lagoons because of hippopotamuses and crocodiles.

Banks

Banks can be found in all cities and towns in South Africa. In the larger cities, most banks open daily from 9.00 a.m. to 3.30 p.m. and on Saturdays from 8.30 a.m. to 11.00 a.m. Subsidiary branches of banks in remote areas may have shorter opening times.

Camping

In South Africa there are around 700 campsites, normally referred to as caravan parks. Almost every larger town has at least one basic-standard Municipal Caravan Park with clean sanitary facilities. Most of the camp grounds in the National Parks, game reserves and wilderness areas are outstanding. It is advisable to book a site in the main season and on public holidays, as the South Africans themselves are keen campers. Camping outside the official sites is not permitted in South Africa. In the vicinity of larger cities or near the coast it is not recommended anyway, for safety reasons. Sometimes, on long trips on small roads, however, one may not have any other choice. But one should always be aware that the wilderness in Africa really can be dangerous.

Camp site and caravan park in Royal Natal National Park.

North of Durban there are many beaches for swimming: this is Umhlanga.

Passports and Visas

For the majority of foreign nationals who travel to South Africa for vacation, entry is straightforward and hassle-free. All visitors to South Africa must be in possession of a valid passport in order to enter the country, and in some cases, a visa. Travelers from certain regions of the world (Scandinavia, Japan, the USA, and most Western European and Commonwealth countries) do not need to apply formally for a visa. Upon arrival in South Africa, visitors from countries falling into this category will automatically be given a free entry permit sticker that outlines how long they may remain in the country. This automatic entry permit is usually for a maximum of 90 days.

Electricity

The electrical voltage in South Africa is 223/230 volts alternating current. Electric sockets require three-pin plugs, for which an adapter should be purchased on arrival, as they are hard to obtain in other countries. In rural areas, electricity may be provided by a generator and voltages may be irregular.

Metropolis at Table Mountain

The Best Walking Tour of Cape Town

From the picturesque old harbor district (Victoria & Alfred Waterfront) you will come to Heerengracht, at the end of which is a park with a monument to the founder of the city, Jan van Riebeeck. Continue into adjoining Adderley Street, the main thoroughfare of Cape Town, to reach the five-cornered Castle of Good Hope, the oldest building in the country (1666-1679), built by whites. Opposite the fortress is a square called Grand Parade, bounded on the other side of Darling Street by the splendid City Hall with its bell tower. This was built in 1905 in the style of the Italian Renaissance. Returning to Adderley Street and continuing straight ahead you will arrive at the Old Town House (1755), built in the Baroque style. It is worthwhile making a detour to Greenmarket Square, where street musicians and painters entertain the public. Across Church Street, with

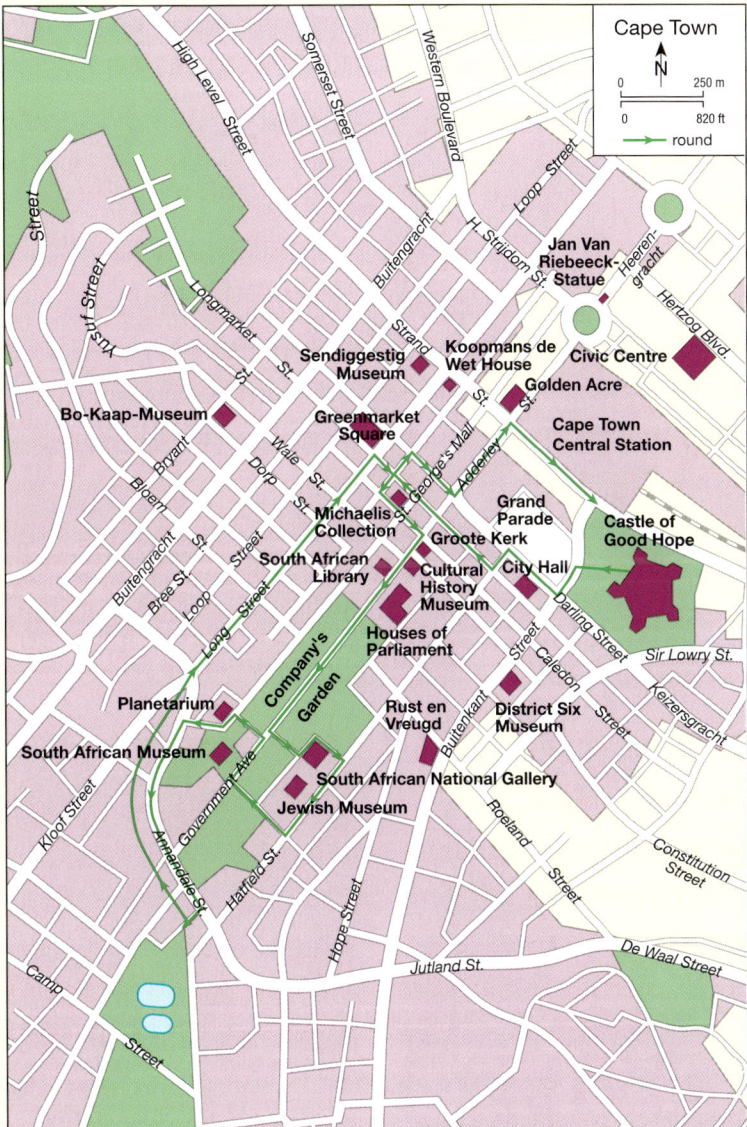

City Hall in Cape Town is built in the style of the Italian Renaissance. The tower is modeled on Big Ben in London (top).
The Old Town House (bottom).

its antique shops, you can return to Adderley Street near the Groote Kerk (1799). The neighboring building, currently the South African Cultural History Museum, was originally used as accommodation for slaves, and later as a post office, a library and the seat of the Supreme Court. At the corner of Wale Street is St. George's Cathedral (1901), built in the Gothic revival style and the former see of Bishop Desmond Tutu (born 1931). Original stones taken from English cathedrals were built into the walls. The next stop is the Houses of Parliament (1814), opposite which stands the South African Library. A copy of every book published in South Africa is filed in the archives. Adderley Street leads directly into the magnificent Government Avenue. Here there are fine buildings such as the South African Museum and the South African National Gallery. Behind you can see the white towers of the Great Synagogue and the unmistakable outline of Table Mountain (1,086 meters/3,563 feet). In the grounds to the left of the National Gallery is the Tynhuis (1751), the official residence of the President. The glorious finale to this walking tour could be to continue along Government Avenue for a visit to the Mount Nelson Hotel on Orange Street, a pastel-colored palace with fascinating old-world charm.

A Wildlife Paradise for Tourists

The Most Beautiful National Parks at a Glance

1

3

2

1 Pelicans can be seen at the Atlantic coast and at Lake Sabaya.
2 Cheetahs can be tamed.
3 Wildebeest (here a herd in Transfrontier Park) are often aptly described as animals with the front body of cattle, the rear body of antelopes and the tail of a horse.
4 The diversity of the animal world in southern Africa is most impressive, especially birds.
5 Yellow-billed hornbill.

In South Africa there are 580 National Parks, Game Parks and private game reserves. They are all maintained by the National Parks Board, with the exception of KwaZulu-Natal, where the Natal Parks Board is responsible. The number of smaller nature reserves administered by provincial governments and private reserves far exceeds that of the National Parks. The nature reserves reflect the diverse landscape of South Africa and range from the isolated Kgalagadi Transfrontier Park (newly founded in 1999, 36,000 sq km/ 13,896 square miles) and the nearby Augrabies Falls National Park (founded in 1966, 820 sq km/ 317 square miles) in the North to the coastal protected areas of Tsitsikamma National Park (founded in 1964, 700 sq km/ 270 square miles) at the Indian Ocean, and from the West Coast National Park on the Atlantic coast (with numerous seabirds) to the National Parks of the Drakensberg in KwaZulu-Natal.

Of the official National Parks, the Kruger National Park (founded in 1898, 19,455 sq km/ 7,510 square miles) is the oldest, and certainly the best known. In 2001, it

became South Africa's second transfrontier megapark (the first was Kgalagadi Transfrontier Park). It now covers an area of 99,000 sq km (38,214 square miles), extending into the states of Mozambique and Zimbabwe. Besides 12 different ecological systems, the visitor can see almost all the varieties of animals, even the rare African wild dog. The endangered black rhinoceros, the emblem of the Natal Parks Board, can best be seen in the Itala Game Reserve (founded in 1972, 300 sq km/ 116 square miles); for an encounter with the white rhinoceros, also threatened with extinction, you should visit the Hluhluwe-Umfolozi Game Reserves (founded in 1895, amalgamated in 1982, 960 sq km/ 371 square miles). The Greater St Lucia Wetlands Park (founded in 1897, 2,750 sq km/ 1,062 square miles) is recommended for observing hippopotamuses and crocodiles. The nyala, the most beautiful of all varieties of antelope and once almost extinct, can best be seen in the Mkuzi Game Reserve (founded in 1912, 250 sq km/ 97 square miles) in which 400 varieties of bird also benefit from optimum conditions. The mountain zebra is at home in Mountain Zebra National Park (65 sq km/ 25 square miles). There are good opportunities for close-up views of elephants in Addo Elephant National Park (150 sq km/ 58 square miles). Bonteboks can be seen in the Bontebok National Park (near Swellendam) and in the Cape of Good Hope Nature Reserve. The rare Big Five can best be seen in the private game reserves near the Kruger National Park and in the Phinda Private Game Reserve (founded in 1992, 170 sq km/ 66 square miles).

In an inaccessible region on the coast of the Indian Ocean, on the border with Mozambique, lies the unspoiled nature reserve of the Sodwana Bay National Park (scuba diving and sand dune hiking), Kosi Bay Nature Reserve, Tembe Elephant Park and Ndumu Game Reserve (bird watching). The latter are for safari freaks who like to avoid the usual tourist routes. Richtersveld National Park (founded in 1991) and lying in an isolated region on the Oranje River at the border with Namibia may only be accessed in a four-wheel-drive vehicle and in a convoy. In a class of their own are the National Parks and game reserves in the Drakensberg, such as the Royal Natal National Park (founded in 1916, 80 sq km/ 31 square miles) or the no less attractive Golden Gate National Park (founded in 1962, 116 sq km/ 45 square miles) near the border with Lesotho, which has impressive red-gold sandstone rock formations. Giant's Castle Game Reserve (founded in 1903, 346 km^2/ 134 square miles) is ideal for longer hiking tours in the mountains.

Getting Around within the Country

Rail: South Africa has an excellent rail network. Passenger trains run between all the larger cities, but even on smaller lines, there are good connections. For longer distances, sleeping cars are available. The Trans Karoo Express connects Johannesburg with Cape Town

On safari in the Hluhluwe Game Reserve.

(daily, length of journey: 24 hours); the Trans Natal Express links Durban with Johannesburg (daily, length of journey 12 hours) and the Trans Oranje Express runs from Cape Town to Durban via Kimberley and Bloemfontein (once a week, length of journey 37 hours). A special experience for tourists is a journey with the Blue Train that runs between Cape Town and Johannesburg/ Pretoria (two or three times a week, length of journey 25 hours). The equally interesting Rovos Rail connects Pretoria with the Kruger National Park. The Apple Express runs between Elizabeth and Avontuur on the longest section of 610 mm gauge railway in the world (every second weekend); the Banana Express from Port Shepstone to Izotsha (Thurs. and Sun.) or to Paddock (Wed. and Sat.). The Shongololo Express travels from Johannesburg to Durban and Durban to Cape Town, and the Outeniqua Choo-Tjoe from George to Knysna (Mon. – Fri.).

Bus: Bus connections between the cities are frequent and one can also travel to Namibia, Botswana and Zimbabwe. A guided bus tour can be booked in advance from overseas. In South Africa, the air-conditioned long-distance buses of Greyhound and Translux Intercity Express (Johannesburg, Durban, Port Elizabeth, Cape Town) and Intercape Mainliner (Cape Town – Windhoek, Johannesburg – Windhoek) can be recommended.

Air: South African Airways (SAA) maintains a close network of flights within southern Africa. In addition, private airlines offer frequent flights to the National Parks.

The Landscape of Vendaland, near the border to Simbabwe.

Taxis/cabs: Taxis must be called from the taxi stands. Prices vary from city to city.

Car Rental: Cars can be booked in advance from overseas from all the international rental companies. The risk of having to wait for a long time because of a breakdown, without obtaining help or being able to reach a repair shop is small in South Africa. Nevertheless, some basic equipment should be on board, for example, a suitable V-belt, tools for changing a wheel (and of course a spare tire). In South Africa, especially at high elevations, it can be very cold. Therefore the car heater should be checked, as well as the air conditioning and cooler fan. Since in tropical regions, day and night are equally long, something should be taken along to use as a blackout (sunrise is shortly after 6.00 a.m.) as well as a gas and petroleum lamp (it gets dark at 6 p.m.). A small fridge in the car is of course very useful for drinks and medication. When renting a vehicle, you should read the small print of the

contract carefully, as insurance conditions may be different from those with which you are familiar. For instance, in the case of accidentally leaving the road due to excess speed, you may be liable for all damage. Rented cars should only be hired with fully comprehensive insurance.

Health Precautions

Especially during the summer, a good sunscreen is very important. It is also essential to drink plenty when the weather is very hot, not least in order to ensure an adequate supply of salt for the body. Prophylactic measures against malaria are urgently recommended for visitors to the Kruger National

A pass road through magnificent mountain scenery: the Outeniqua Mountains.

Museums

Museums are generally open Mon. to Fri. from 9.00 a.m. – 5.00 p.m. and on weekends from 10.00 a.m. – 4.00 p.m.

National Parks

In 1657, only five years after the founding of Cape Town, the governor of the Dutch East India Company, Jan van Riebeeck, issued the first restrictions on hunting for the protection of wild animals in South Africa. Nevertheless, it was not possible to prevent giraffes and elephants from being almost wiped out, and the zebra-like quagga and the Cape lion from becoming extinct. The new rendering of the National Parks Act (1976) extend-

Park and KwaZulu-Natal. Tablets can be obtained without prescription in all pharmacies. Other vaccinations are not required for South Africa. You should never swim in lakes or rivers, as bilharzia is widespread, especially in the eastern regions of the country.

Clothing

Clothing should be suitable for a warm, moderate climate, that is, light and airy. Cotton is the fabric of choice. However, in South Africa there are large differences between day and night temperatures. For the cooler evenings, and especially for journeys in mountainous areas, a light sweater is essential, and also a jacket or parka should not be forgotten. In the game reserves and when hiking one should wear subdued colors, so as not to be easily visible to the animals; furthermore, flies and insects are attracted to bright colors. Generally, clothing can be informal, but a jacket and tie should be taken for hotel stays. An umbrella and good shoes are also essential equipment.

Traveling with Children

Private tour operators and bush camps only permit children on their safaris who are at least four years of age. Some operators offer

The South African Museum in Cape Town, in the background, the Jesuit church.

all kinds of entertainment for children (seven to nine years and older) without their parents. And apart from that, South Africa is one of the most child-friendly countries on the continent of Africa.

ed protection to "landscapes of great esthetic beauty" (for example, parts of the Drakensberg) and cultural heritage monuments (for example, the rock drawings of the San). In addition a whole series of

Discovering the Land at the Cape

The Five Most Scenic Routes

Rocky cliffs in the Drakensberg in Mpumalanga.

Route 1: The Coastal Route

At the Cape of Good Hope.

This is the "tourist route" of South Africa par excellence, as it is in the programs of almost all tour operators. It leads from Cape Town along an incredibly beautiful coast to popular vacation resorts frequented by the inhabitants of Cape Town. In the Cape region, as well as between Cape Town and Mossel Bay, the traveler will find an abundance of attractive wine estates. The journey continues through a land of picture-book lagoons and fine sand beaches between Mossel Bay and Plettenberg Bay. The next highlight comes in the picturesque rainforest (Tsitsikamma) and the enchanting villages offering culinary delights, such as the oyster town of Knysna. From George you can make a detour into the unique Little Karoo and visit the Cango Caves with their stalactites and the ostrich farms near Oudtshoorn. This eventful trip with many scenic high points ends with a visit to Addo Elephant National Park. Tourists normally fly from Port Elizabeth to Durban, thus avoiding the trip through the former Transkei, a route that is reputed to be dangerous.

Route 2: Through the Mountains and the Game Reserves of Zululand

A journey to the "barrier of raised spears," as the Zulu named the Drakensberg in Natal, is one of the unforgettable experiences of a visit to South Africa. The starting point is Durban. Approach the mountain region via Pietermaritzburg and the impressive Howick Falls. A visit to KwaZulu-Natal should also include a visit to the Valley of 1000 Hills, the Zulu settlements and the battlefields where the infamous battles between the Boers, British and Zulus took place. The next highlights are the game reserves with their huge diversity of species, such as the Hluhluwe-Umfolozi game reserves, the Mzuke and St Lucia reserves, or the private Itala and Phinda Game Reserves that are among the most beautiful in South Africa. This route is certainly the most colorful one.

Traditional round Zulu farmsteads and modern square houses.

Route 3: The Panorama Route

The trip to the Blyde River Canyon and the Kruger National Park in Mpumulanga Province is a must on the list of every visitor to South Africa. It can be combined with a visit to the Northern Province, the land of the smaller Bantu peoples, the Venda, Tsonga, Bechuana and Shona that is seldom offered in organized tours. The journey begins in Johannesburg and leads via Pretoria past the foothills of the Magalies Mountains through the typical highveld to the Soutspansberg Mountains. The land of the Rain Queen where the white python-god is revered boasts pretty small towns like Tzaneen and Louis Trichardt. The landscape becomes dramatic when the Transvaal Drakensberg drop steeply from their most northerly point into the dry plain of the bushveld. At the edge of the steep slope, the Panorama Route follows the Blyde River. The descent from the rugged slopes to the game-filled Kruger National

Another choice would be from Johannesburg via Kimberley, the former Eldorado of the diamond industry, to the Kalahari Park. As a rule, you take the route from Cape Town through the Namaqua Desert to Clanwilliam at the foot of the Cedarberg Mountains and

Gate of rock at Golden Gate National Park.

Park is crowned by the transition from the highveld to the subtropical lowveld, with its acacia and mopane forests. This is the route with the most interesting scenery.

Bizarrely shaped: a quiver tree.

Route 4: The Boer Route

This route begins in Johannesburg – after Cape Town, the most important metropolis of South Africa. Traveling southwest, after crossing the gently rolling grasslands of the former Boer Republic and passing Kroonstad, you enter the impressive world of the pasturelands and their enormous farms. The "Gold Province" is, of course, famous for its gold mines and its historic tradition. The capital city of the Free State, Bloemfontein, has numerous interesting sights. From here, it can be worth making a detour to the Kingdom of Lesotho, parallel to the South African border, or a journey to Ficksburg and Bethlehem, and then continuing to the Golden Gate Highlands National Park, famous for its scenic beauty at the northern end of the Natal Drakensberg. Along the way, the scenic impressions are unique among their kind.

Route 5: The Desert Route

This route is recommended for travelers who have sufficient time and a taste for adventure and who are looking for an authentic experience of nature. It leads from Cape Town northwards towards the border with Namibia and to the Kgalagadi Transfrontier Park (the more interesting variant).

continue northwards to Springbok, and then eastwards through the Upper Karoo to the Augrabies Falls. At the intersection of these two variants lies the "Afrikaner town" of Upington, directly on the banks of the Oranje River. Passing red sand dunes from which the wind entices gentle tones (Roaring Dunes), you finally reach the Kgalagadi Transfrontier Park, one of the most impressive national parks in the country, situated in the arid landscape of the Kalahari. This route is the most uncomfortable, but undoubtedly includes the most spectacular landscapes.

153

Buffalo are the epitome of concentrated strength. They are always accompanied by tick birds.

private game reserves has been set up. Today, South Africa has some of the most up-to-date nature and animal protection legislation in Africa. The ideal time to visit is generally the months from August to October. For game watching, the transition between the southern winter and the southern spring is advisable, because the animals stay close to the waterholes and the grass is still low.

Reservations can be made at South African National Parks, PO Box 787, Pretoria 0001;
tel. +27/(0)12/3431991,
fax +27/(0)12/3430905,
reservations@parks-sa.co.za
Website: www.sanparks.org
(bookings for the Golden Gate, Kgalagadi, Kruger, Tsitsikamma, Addo and Augrabies National Parks).
KwaZulu-Natal Nature Conservation, PO Box 13069, Cascades 3203, tel. +27/(0)33/8451000, fax +27/(0)33/8451001 (bookings for Giant's Castle, Greater St Lucia, Hluhluwe-Umfolozi, Royal Natal and Itala Parks).

Postal Services

Postal services are generally good. At main post offices, a general delivery (poste restante) service is usually available.
Opening times: Mon., Tues., Thurs., Fri 8.30 a.m. – 4.30 p.m., Wed. 9.00 a.m. – 4.40 p.m., Sat. 8.00 a.m. – 12 noon.

Safety

South Africa is by and large not a dangerous destination for travelers, but the same precautions apply as in other developing countries. For example, as far as possible it is advisable to keep away from lonely regions and avoid large crowds of people (as in railway stations and at markets); make a copy of all travel documents, leave money in a safe and do not carry large sums of cash around on your person. Under no circumstances should you flash your wealth around. Furthermore, the high murder rate (although it is bad enough) is restricted to Johannesburg and the slum districts of the other large urban settlements. Frightening reports of shootings and riots generally affect only local people and areas that tourists will not be visiting anyway. However, visitors from Europe or North America should be warned of the dangers in wilderness areas, as they often tend

Black rhinos are more aggressive than white rhinos.

to underestimate these. Not only the big cats are wild animals, but also the zebras that are grazing outside the lodge or baboons lying in wait for prey near the camp grounds can cause serious injuries with kicks or bites. It seems incredible, but newspapers in South Africa once reported that a group of Japanese who were visiting a National Park left their vehicle to take a photograph of themselves in front of a group of lions. The result was as sad as it was predictable.

Souvenirs

All kinds of carvings typical of the different tribes are especially popular souvenirs, as well as other hand-crafted products, leather goods, pictures and pottery. Sports articles and safari clothing are also good value in South Africa. Colorful knitted sweaters and attractive shawls and scarves woven from mohair wool are made in Lesotho. The best place for purchasing silk fabrics is Durban. For many visitors, South Africa is the land of gold and diamonds and of semi-precious stones. Trade in antiques (furniture and jewelry) is booming at present, particularly in Johannesburg and Cape Town. For amounts above 250 South African rand, overseas visitors can claim back the sales tax they have paid on presentation of the appropriate receipts. This reimbursement must be claimed at the airport.

Simon's Town is characterized by beautiful colonial buildings.

Telephone Calls

The national phone code for South Africa from overseas is 0027, for Lesotho 00266, for Swaziland 00268. The outgoing code is 00 followed by the relevant country code (e.g. 0044 for the United Kingdom). There are area codes for the different cities, for example, 021 for Cape Town and 011 for Johannesburg. A special feature is that some numbers begin with 0020 – these calls go through a switchboard. Using hotel telephones is the most expensive option, as they charge according to whim. The international code (as of January 2007) for the UK is: 00 44, for USA: 00 1.

Telephone calls abroad can be made from the blue coin-operated telephones; card phones are green. As of 8 January 2007, South Africa has changed to 10-digit dialling, so city codes must be included e.g. 021 for Cape Town). The international dialling code has changed from 09 to 00. International phone cards cannot be used in South Africa. The country is served by three GSM mobile phone networks. Mobile service providers offer very cheap 'pay-as-you-go' Sim cards, which are a good option for visitors staying for some time. Internet cafes are widespread.
Police and fire brigade: 10111, accident 10177, inquiries 1025.

Tipping

Tipping is practiced much as in other countries. In a restaurant, it is customary to add 10 to 15 percent of the amount to the bill; taxi drivers receive 10 percent. Porters and hotel maids receive 3 rand.

Accommodation

The types of accommodation that are available are as diverse as the country itself. Many of the more exclusive hotels belong to a large hotel chain. Self-catering accommodation is available in various categories: these may be cottages, chalets, bungalows or rondavels. The popular accommodation choice in private houses offers personal attention and Bed and Breakfast. In the country, there are vacation farms where guests may stay in a farmhouse. Lodges on the private game reserves are expensive, but generally organize excellent safaris. In the National Parks,

The Mont-aux-Sources – a beautiful hotel resort in Royal Natal National Park.

the rest camps offer simple but comfortable accommodation in the form of bungalows or chalets. Campsites can be quite noisy at night, but they often have shopping facilities, a restaurant, swimming pool and sometimes even tennis courts or a bowling alley.

Currency

The currency of South Africa is the South African rand. It is also accepted in Swaziland and Lesotho. One rand is divided into 100 cents. Approximate exchange rates:
1 Euro = approximately 6.26 rand;

Tree in the Kgalagadi Transfrontier Park.

1 US$ = approximately 4.81 rand; 1 Pound Sterling (UK) = 14.15 Rand International credit cards are generally accepted. Travelers' checks in common currencies can be exchanged in all banks.

Customs Duties

One liter of spirits or 2 liters of wine, 400 cigarettes and 50 cigars may be imported into the country duty-free. For weapons, a permit is essential and for animals, of course, the relevant import license. Gifts up to a value of 200 Euro (approx. US$ 250) may be taken out of the country. In accordance with the regulations of the Convention on Biological Diversity for the protection of endangered species, trade with endangered animals or plants is strictly regulated; these items may be confiscated.

People, Places, Topics

Italic page numbers refer to photos.

People

Afrikaners, cf Boers 16

Baker, Sir Herbert 51, 107
Bantu 17, 78, 90, 152
Basotho *27*, *32*, 90
Bennett, George 66
Boers 16, 25, 45, 52, 80, 91, 96, 100, 107–109, 116, 118 f., 131, 144, 152
Breda, Michiel van 54
Broom, Robert 17
Bushman, cf San 16, 86, 87, 129

Women pounding millet in a Zulu kraal.

Cetshwayo 96
Chapman, John 43
Cilliers, Sarel *119*
Clanwilliam, Earl of 130

d'Almeida, Francisco 20, 23
d'Urban, Sir Benjamin 85
Dart, Raymond 17

Dias, Bartolomeu 20, 23, 25, 62, 74
Dingane 94
Dingiswayo 94
Donkin, Sir Rufane 74
Drake, Sir Francis *43*, 23

Elizabeth II 74

Gama, Vasco da 20, 23, 85
Gandhi, Mahatma 20, 86
Gardiner, Allen Francis 85
George III 63, 67
Graham, John 82

Haggard, Henry Rider 108
Herero *122*, 142
Himba (Namibia) *26*, *136*, 143
Hobhouse, Emily 45, 119
Hottentots cf Khoikhoi
Houtman, Cornelius de 62
Huguenots 20, 25, *50*, 52, 55, 58
Jakobs, Stephanus Erasmus 124

Janszen, Leendert 23, 40
João II 23
Joubert, Piet 78

Khoikhoi 16 f., 20, 22, 40, 62, 65, 67, 72, 129, 136
Klerk, Frederik Willem de 21, *21*, 30
Kruger, Paul (»Ohm«) 107, *107*, 112

Lightfoot, Hannah 67
Lindequist, Friedrich von 143
Livingstone, David 122
Livingstone, Mary 129
Lobengula 78
Louis XIV 52, 58

Magomo *21*
Malan, Rian 105
Mandela, Nelson *21*, 21, 30, 42, 104, 113
Mbandzeni 100
Mbeki, Thabo Mvuyelwa 21
Mhlangane 94
Moffat, Robert 129
Moshoeshoe I. 91
Mswazi II. 100

Ndebele *12*, *78*, 78 f., 108
Nongqawuse 84
Nyabela 78

Pigg, William 101
Plettenberg, Joachim van 72
Potgieter, Piet 108, 116
Pretorius, Andries 96

Reitz, Frederick 119
Retief, Piet 95
Rex, George 67
Rhodes, Cecil 15, *20*, 78
Riebeeck, Jan van *22*, 25, 40, 47, 58, 147, 151
Rose, Max 70
Saldanha, Antonio de 23

San woman in the Kalahari.

San *10*, 16, 22, 86, 90, 92, 129, 11, 138, 151, *156*,
Sandile *21*
Schreiner, Olive 15
Schroeder, Christiaan Wilhelm H. 137
Senzangakona 94
Shaka Zulu 25, 85, 90, 94
Shona 22, 152
Stel, Simon van der 42, 44, 47, 58
Stevenson-Hamilton, James 113
Swazi 78, *100*, 100
Swellengrebel, Hendrik 54

Tolkien, John Ronald Reuel 72
Tonga 97
Tutu, Desmond 16, 42, 104, 147

Upington, Sir Thomas 137

Voortrekker 95, 106 f., 108

Xhosa 20, 25, *27*, 42, 78, 80, 80, 82, 82, 84, 84 f.

Zulu 15, *11*, *12*, 25, *26*, *29*, 78, 80, 86, *94*, 94–97, *98*, 100, 107, 145, 145, 152, *152*, *156*

156

Places and Topics

Acacia 38, 139, 153
Addo Elephant National Park 6f, 74, 75, *134*, 149, 52, 154
Aloe *93*, *139*
Amphitheater *52*, *86*, 87, 92
Antelope *34*, 74, 86, 97, *129*, 149
Apartheid 21, 26, 30, 42, 54, 91, 101, 107, 116, 119
Architecture *24*, 47, 50, 54, 74, 157
Augrabies Falls *5*, *125*, 136, 144, 153
Augrabies Falls National Park 131, 136, 148, 154
Barrydale *63*, *63*
Battlefields 95, 152
Berlin Falls *116*, 116
Bourke's Luck Potholes 114, *114*
Bredasdorp 54, 157
Brenton-on-Sea 67, 73
Buffalo 30, 74, 96, 112, 134, 135, 154
Buffalo City 82
Buffels Bay 66, 72
Bushveld 15, 38, 152

Caledon *60*
Caledon River 90
Calvinia 130
Camping 12, 85, 118, 126, 146, 155
Cango Caves 65, 152
Cape Agulhas 17, 55
Cape Cross *142*
Cape of Good Hope 12, 23, 25, 44, 46, 152

Boschendal: an insider tip for fans of Cape Dutch architecture.

Bethlehem 93, 118, 153
Big Five *5*, *134*, 134 f., 149
Bloemfontein (Manguang) 24, 45, 72, 118 f., *119*, 146, 153
Blood River 25, 96, 108
Blyde River *32*, *38*, *114*, 114, 116, 152
Blyde River Canyon *11*, *103*, *114*, 152
Boer Trek *23*
Boer War 15, 20, 26, 45, 74, 82, 100, 118
Bokspits *124*, 138
Bontebok National Park 149
Bophuthatswana 31, 116
Boschendal *50*, *54*, 54, *56*, 157
Botshabelo *78*, 79
Botswana 15, 101, 122 f., *122*, 138, 144, 150
Bottle Tree 138

Cape of Good Hope Nature Reserve cf Cape of Good Hope 44, 149
Cape Town 10, 14, 20, *20*, 22, 22, 25, 38, 40, 42, *41*, 44, 46, 47, *51*, 51, 54, 58, 62, 67, 106, 124, 126, 144–148, *147*, 150, 151, 152–155
Cathedral Rock 84
Cathkin Peak 86
Cedarberg Mountains 126, 128, 130, 153
Cedarberg Wilderness Area 126
Ceres 126
Cheetahs 96, 112, 113, 123, 148
Chobe National Park 122
Ciskei 26, 31, 82, 83
Citrusdal 126
Clanwilliam 126, 130, 153
Clifton Bay *46*
Coffee Bay 84
Constantia 47, 58

Cradock 15
Cuisine 28

Damaraland *142*
Drakensberg (Mpumalanga) *32*, 39, 109, 144, *152*
Drakensberg Mountains (KwaZulu) *5*, 15, 25, 86, 90, 94, 148, 151
Dundee 96
Durban 11, *23*, *28*, 25, 62, 80, 85, *85*, 94, *96*, 144, 146, *146*, 149, 152, 158

East London (Buffalo City) 80, 82, 84, 146
Echo Caves 22
Elephant 1, 33, 74, 96, 134 f., *134*, 149, 151
Epupa Waterfalls *12*, *32*, 143
Etosha National Park *113*, 143, 158
Ezulweni 101

Ficksburg 153
Fish Hoek 22
Folklore 102
Fort Frederick 74
Fort Selwyn 82
Franschhoek 20, *50*, *50*, 52, 55, 58
Free State 153

Garden Route 10, 39, 60–63, 65–67, *66*, 73, 80, 144
George 63, 64, 65, 152
Giant's Castle Game Reserve 86, 87, 149, 154
God's Window 114, 117
Gold Reef City *104*
Golden Gate Highlands National Park 18, *92*, 93, 149, 153
Goukamma Nature Reserve 66
Graaff Reinet 15, 25, 65, 96
Grahamstown *50*, 51, 80, 82, *82*
Great Brak River *66*
Great Karoo 16, 65
Great Kei River 80, 83
Great Limpopo Transfrontier Park 113
Greater Kudu 158
Greater St. Lucia Wetland Park 97, 149, 152, 154
Groenenkloof *20*
Groot Constantia Wine Estate 59
Groot River Mouth 72
Gudu Falls 92

Hazyview 116
Hermanus 54, 62
Hibiscus Coast 85
Highveld 38, 90, 109, 144, 152
Hippopotamus 31, 97, 149
Hluhluwe Umfolozi Reserve 30, 96, *96*, 134, 149, 150, 152, 154
Hole in the Wall 84
Homelands 26, 31
Hotagterklip 16, *17*
Howick Falls 86, 152
Humansdorp 60, 73, 80

Idutywa *82*
Islandhlwana 96
Itala Game Reserve 97, 149, 152, 154

Jeffrey's Bay 73, 74, 80
Johannesburg 17, *23*, *28*, 30, 102–107, 118, 145 f., 150, 152–155

Kaaimans River 63, 65, 68
Kagga Kamma 129
Kakamas 127, 131
Kalahari 5, 15, 38, 123, 128, 130, *134*, *138*, 138, *143*, 153, *156*
Kaókoland/Kaókoveld 143, *136*
Karoo Nature Reserve 38
Kei River 83
Keimoes 127, 131
Kenhardt 131
Kgalagadi Transfrontier Park 36, 138, 144, 148, 153, 155
Kimberley 17, 20, 45, 70, 124, 126, 146, 152

Church in Bredasdorp.

King William's Town 80
Kirstenbosch Botanical Gardens 14, 44, 53
Klasies River Mout Caves 22
Knysna 39, 65 ff., 73, 152
Kookerboom Forest 124, 131
Kosi Bay Nature Reserve 149
Kroonstad 45, 118, 119, 153
Kruger Nationalpark 11, 22, 100, 112 f., 112, 118,
135, 144, 14, 150, 152, 154, 159
Kwa Bhekithunga 98
Kwandebele 79
KwaZulu-Natal 26, 39, 90, 91, 100, 106, 144, 148, 150, 152

Lake District 66
Lake Sabaya 148
Lebombo Mountains 100
Leopard 5, 90, 101, 112, 131, 134, 135, 144, 146, 154
Lesotho 32, 86, 90, 93, 149, 153
Letaba River 109
Letchwe antelope 122
Lions 32 f., 134, 134, 151
Lisbon Falls 116
Little Karoo 4, 34, 59, 62 f., 62, 64, 70, 152
Lobamba Royal Village 101
Long-Tom-Pass 118, 118
Loopspruit 79, 79
Louis Trichardt 108, 152, 154

The Vasco da Gama clock in Durban.

Lowveld 16, 109, 117, 118, 144
Lydenburg 20, 100, 118

MacMac Falls 116, 117
Makapan 17
Maluti Mountains 93
Maun 122, 122
Mbabane 101
Middelburg 79
Mkuzi Game Reserve 149, 152
Montagu 4, 34, 59
Mont-aux-Sources 87
Moremi Game Reserve 122, 123
Mosambique 113, 144, 149
Mossel Bay 60, 62, 64, 152
Mountain Zebra National Park 15, 149
Mpako River 84
Mpumalanga 86, 152

Namaqualand 16, 38 f., 126, 130
Namib Desert 10, 142, 143
Namibia 12, 21, 32, 38, 123, 136, 139, 140, 142, 149 f., 153, 158, 159
Natal 20, 25, 39, 85, 90, 94, 96, 109
Ndumu Game Reserve 149
Nossob River 138

Okavango 122, 122
Olifants River 59, 114, 130, 153
Oranje 20, 25, 38, 118
Oranje River 5, 45, 91, 125, 131, 136, 149
Oribi Gorge Nature Reserve 94
Ostrich 28, 65, 70, 70 f., 130, 152
Oudtshoorn 65, 71, 152
Outeniqua Choo-Tjoe 65, 68, 150
Outeniqua Pass/Mountains 63, 64, 151

Paarl 20, 52, 54, 58
Palisander 14
Panorama Route 114, 116, 117, 152
Phinda Reservat 29, 97, 97, 149, 152
Piet Retief 55
Pietermaritzburg 86, 86, 152
Pigg's Peak 101, 101
Pinnacle Rock 116
Plettenberg Bay 62, 72, 74, 152
Port Edward 83, 85, 146
Port Elizabeth 22, 60, 73, 74, 80, 150, 152
Pretoria 14, 26, 79, 79, 86, 102, 106, 146, 150, 152
Prince Albert 65
Protea 14, 38, 39, 73, 126, 126, 158

Greater kudu antelope in Etosha National Park

Qiloane Waterfall 91
Quiver tree 38, 124, 131, 153
Qwaqwa Mountains 80, 92, 92

Rainbow Nation 16, 26, 45
Ramskop 130
Rhebokskloof 34, 59
Rhinoceros 96, 97, *134*, 134, 149, 154
Richtersveld 16, 149
Robben Island 42, *42*
Royal Natal National Park 81, 86, 87, 88, 146, 149, 154, 155

Sabie Game Reserve 113
Sani Pass 90, 91
Sedgefield 65
Settler's Country 80
Sharpeville 21, 31, 145
Simonstown 44, 52, 155
Sossusvlei 140, 142
Soweto 21, 30, 104, 145
Stellenbosch 20, 24, 25, 34, 47, 54
Sterkfontein 17
Storms River 17, 60, 73, 76
Sun City 116
Sunshine Coast 85
Swaziland 15, 100, 100, 144, 146, 155
Swellendam 25, 48, 54, 63, 149

Taung 17
Tiger Falls 92
Transkei 26, 31, 38, 82, 83, 152
Transvaal 20, 24, 26, 78, 100, 152
Treur River 114, 116
Tsitsikamma National Park/Forest 39, 62, 72, 144, 46, 148, 152, 154

Tulbagh 126
Twyfelfontein 143
Tzaneen 109, 152

Ulundi 96
Umfolozi 97
Umhlanga 146
Umkomanazana River Valley 96
Umtata 83
Upington 126 f., 131, 137, 144, 153

Valley of 1000 Hills 11, 94, 94, 150, 152
Venda 31, 108
Vredendal 126, 130

Waterbuck 6, 112
West Coast National Park 148
Whales 46, 54, 62, 84
White River 28
Wildcoast 39, 82 f., 85
Wildebeest 6, 112, 128, 148
Wilderness 4, 61, 65
Wine estate 10, 44, 50, 52, 54, 56, 58, 152
Wine growing 12, 47, 52, 58, 63, 63

Yellow-billed hornbill 149

Zebra 31, 33, 97, 112, 149, 154
Zimbabwe 113, 144, 149

A baboon in the Kruger National Park (right-hand page).

www.bucher-publishing.com

Experience the colors of our world

Mongolia
ISBN 978-3-7658-1627-7
ordering code 81627

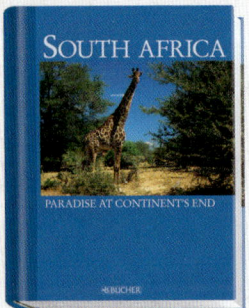

South Africa
ISBN 978-3-7658-1626-0
ordering code 81626

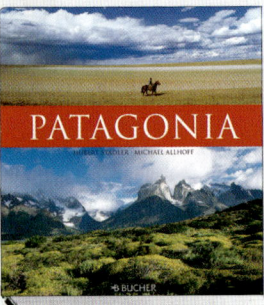

Patagonia
ISBN 978-3-7658-1590-4
ordering code 81590

Little Polar Bears
ISBN 978-3-7658-1586-7
ordering code 81586

Text and Picture Credits Imprint

The author and photographer

Rainer Waterkamp is a political scientist. He studied media science in Berlin and worked in public relations for local and regional authorities, as well as for the German Federal Government. He headed departments in the fields of image, film and television. For many years, he has traveled in countries outside Europe and his travel reports have been published by well-known newspapers such as "Die Welt," "FAZ," "Frankfurter Rundschau" and several journals.
He has authored travel guides on Ethiopia, the Andes, East Africa and South Africa and published illustrated books. He lives in Bonn, Germany.
E-mail: Rainer.Waterkamp@t-online.de

Cover photos
Front: Giraffe in Kruger-National Park (large photo);
Back: The Outeniqua Choo-Tjoe, bridge over the Kaaimans River

Picture Credits

Africana-Museum, Johannesburg: p. 22; DPA, Frankfurt: p. 21 right. (2); Photo archive C.J. Bucher Verlag, Munich, Germany: p. 23 (4); Peter Hirth, Leipzig: 58 left. (2), 70 (2), 71 top right

We would like to express our gratitude to all copyright owners for their kind permission for reprinting and publishing. In spite of intensive efforts, it has not been possible to establish all copyright owners. We would request these to contact the publisher.

All other photographs are by Rainer Waterkamp.

This work has been carefully researched by the author and kept up to date as well as checked by the publisher for coherence. However, the publishing house can assume no liability for the accuracy of the data contained herein.

We are always grateful for suggestions and advice. Please send your comments to:
C.J. Bucher Publishing,
Product Management
Innsbrucker Ring 15
81673 Munich
Germany
E-mail:
editorial@bucher-publishing.com
Homepage:
www.bucher-publishing.com

Translation:
Janet Mayer, Bruchsal, Germany
Proof-reading:
Jane Michael, Munich, Germany
Graphic design: graphitecture book, Rosenheim, Germany,
revised by Agnes Meyer-Wilmes, Munich, Germany
Cartography: Astrid Fischer-Leitl, Munich, Germany

Product management for the German edition: Joachim Hellmuth
Product management for the English edition: Dr. Birgit Kneip
Production: Bettina Schippel
Repro: Repro Ludwig,
Zell am See, Austria
Printed in Slovenia by MKT Print, Ljubljana

See our full listing of books at
www.bucher-publishing.com

© 2007 C.J. Bucher Verlag GmbH, Munich
All rights reserved. No part of this publication may be reprinted or reproduced, stored in a retrieval system, or transmitted in any form or by any means without prior permission in written form from the publisher.

ISBN 978-3-7658-1626-0